Gardening:
A Growing
Addiction

Gardening: A Growing Addiction

Jo Ann Wiblin

 iUniverse®

GARDENING: A GROWING ADDICTION

iUniverse books may be ordered through booksellers or by contacting:

iUniverse
1663 Liberty Drive
Bloomington, IN 47403
www.iuniverse.com
844-349-9409

ISBN: 978-1-6632-2103-2 (sc)
ISBN: 978-1-6632-2132-2 (e)

Library of Congress Control Number: 2021908259

Print information available on the last page.

iUniverse rev. date: 04/29/2021

PROLOGUE

I have always been interested in plants. My grandparents were avid vegetable gardeners, and when they came to our place to plant, I was right behind them.

After marriage, my mother-in-law often came out to help in our garden, teaching me as we went. As our family grew, I had time to take the Master Gardener's program, and they encouraged us to spread our knowledge to the community. We did, and often.

As a writer and English teacher, I decided to propose a weekly column to the Newark Advocate. They accepted, and it led to 3 1/2 years of weekly columns. The result of that is this book. Understand that the chapters will be rotated by the seasons. Ohio, by the way, has four seasons…..

I hope you not only learn from this effort, but that you laugh with me.

PS. You will see that pruning is one of my passions. I hope it becomes yours too!

For many sunshiny days -

Jo Ann Wiblin

GARDENING STARTED OUT in my life innocently enough. As a child, I followed Grandpa around his garden, once finding peanuts buried under plants there. (They were peanut plants.) Another time, Grandma gave me some tiger lilies to plant, and when our backyard flooded, the lilies were the only things visible above the water. My brother and I, back when we both could fit into the hammock, often shared it with dishpans: the last full of beautiful green peas ready for the kitchen, another with discarded pods, and one filling with peas as we worked. A generation later, I tended my own garden while my babies sat in the swing at the end of the rows. As they grew older, my attention turned to them and their activities, and my garden grew smaller for a while.

As every parent knows, children eventually grow up and go away. Soon, my long-neglected yard and vegetable garden began to call. My husband built a potting bench beneath the pines, and I had a place to store my pots and potting soil. I discovered that it was an excellent place for a plant nursery, with pine needles nestling around the pots and dappled shade protecting the young shoots. Eventually, I convinced my husband that I needed a cold frame. He willingly complied. (He is my chief enabler in this addiction.) Bedding plants no longer cluttered the kitchen from February through May, and he had his place back at the kitchen table for breakfast. But the cold frame only whetted my appetite for more. The following year, my gardening disease became a full-blown addiction. In March, a newly retired friend announced to us at church that he was building a greenhouse. He had found some plans on the internet designed with inexpensive materials and ease of construction. Little did I realize the effect on my life this would have.

Several weeks later, my exhausted husband and I stood in the middle of a 12x16' greenhouse. Even though it was early summer I started flats of seeds. Every morning at daylight, I ran up the hill with my dog Missy to inspect the flats, coffee cup in hand. Several days later, a pale green haze appeared on one of the flats.

Now I had something to keep me busy. I worked daily thinning and potting on the seedlings for an hour or so, the quickest hour of the day. As I worked, Missy snuffled around the tables, sometimes coming out with cobwebs on her face. (Potting on means moving seedlings to larger pots as needed.)

The plants were a beautiful deep green with sturdy stems, not thin and leaning to the light as my kitchen-grown seedlings had been. Soon, roots protruded from the bottom of the containers. My small garden wouldn't hold them all, so friends and neighbors benefitted, if they promised to return the flats.

Next, I graduated to cuttings. Pruning shears and plastic bags in hand, I cruised the yard, snipping anything interesting. Actually, everything was interesting. Hydrangeas, sedums, japonicas, rhododendrons, clematis, even pachysandra all felt the sting of my knife and the cooling mist of my propagation bench. My husband teased me about my impatience to see those roots. He joked that I was constantly uncovering the cuttings to see what was happening. I was, but I denied it.

Two weeks later, I let out a whoop of celebration when I saw two tiny new leaves on the hydrangeas. Ever so gently, I dug them out of the cuttings pot. I placed a golf ball-sized clump of dirt held together by strong white roots in a new pot and put it back on the bench to adjust. I begged my husband to come see my new plants. Did he know that I had paid $29.95 for the original plant? Now I had two, and two more coming!

Second and third rounds of cuttings rooted and grew on in the greenhouse, while I learned a great deal about managing the process. Soon I needed a new source of plants. I took to carrying sandwich bags in the car for emergencies, and one finally occurred at a roadside rest stop next to I-77. There by the walk was Coreopsis Moonbeam going to seed. I quickly pulled off three seeds and slipped them into the bag. In the car, I labeled and dated the bag. Back at home, I discovered beautiful black seeds in my Stella D'Oro plants and on top of my onions. Funny how I had never noticed those seed pods before.

At a friend's wedding in another town while standing in line outside, I took two small cuttings from a beautiful hedge at the church, stuck it in a sandwich bag, and gave it a drink at the water fountain. (I know - I should have asked permission!) Back home I placed it on the propagation bench with a label, "Kevin and July, Aug 2. 1998". It looks as it if will make it. If it does, I plan to give it to the groom's parents. Or maybe I'll keep it and start another for them. I can't decide.

The compulsion is growing. At work in my office, I think of what I should be doing in the greenhouse. Meals, less frequent now, often consist almost entirely of produce from our garden. I need a support group. "My name is Jo Ann, and I am a gardener…"

PRUNING: A MISSION OF MERCY

I love to prune trees. It's a way to direct their growth, prevent their over-crowded and criss-crossing growth, and open up the tree to air and sunshine. Call it compulsive, call it power hungry, call it whatever you want to call it.

I have three pairs of pruning shears, one in the garage, one in the kitchen, and one in the greenhouse. For larger branches, I use loppers. Those are like giant pruning shears, big enough to cut medium-sized branches. For higher branches, we have a pruner on a long pole with a rope to operate the cutting part. I never climb to prune. It's not really safe unless you can stand on the ground to do it. Professionals have the equipment to protect themselves and liability insurance to protect you.

This year, I bought a holster to put on a belt for my pruners. I actually strut around the place wearing it and snipping things. Now that's power!

About this time of year I get that urge. I don't know if it's the proper time, but it's when all the sprouts and suckers show up on the trees. The time to prune is when it's needed, so that's what I do. Some people are afraid to prune, but once you realize that it actually improves the plant and you learn how to improve the plant, it feels like a mission of mercy.

Suckers can be new shoots growing between two branches, or along the base of a branch or the tree. By sprouts I mean the ones growing straight up from a branch. You don't want sprouts at all. Imagine when that sprout gets about 4" in diameter. It would interfere with all the other branches it's crossing as it grows straight up, and will destroy the openness and architecture of the tree. Cut all sprouts and suckers out.

While you're pruning, take a second to cut the smaller branches up into small pieces and put them in a bucket for the compost pile.

So what to cut? Let's imagine a small tree. First, never trim the leader. That's the main stem (trunk) of the tree, unless you really want it to stop growing, which usually you don't.

Second, never remove more than one-third of the branches at one time. That would shock the tree and cause severe damage.

Third, cut off all the suckers around the base of the tree, and along the trunk up to the lowest branch. By the way, where is the lowest branch? It will never get any higher than it is right now, so if you want to get your riding mower or child under it, remove a few lower branches every year, until it is high enough. It's a lot easier to remove them when they're small, rather than hiring a crew to cut off a huge branch years from now.

Next, look for any branches that cross each other. These will eventually rub, causing damage and disease. Pick the one you want to keep, and remove the other one. Finally, look for any broken or damaged branches and remove them.

You should already see a much-improved branch structure.

Next come the more difficult decisions. You will see some branches joining the tree at a 90 degree angle, (an L, for example), the strongest joint. A branch that joins at a narrow angle (a Y) will eventually split in a storm, or under the weight of snow and ice. Remove the branch with the narrow angle.

The rest is art. The goal is to open up the middle of the tree to let in air and light. Think about a robin being able to fly straight through the tree. It will look a little bare at first, but will soon fill in with leaves and small branches.

I expect to see a lot of healthy, attractive trees soon!

ALL QUESTIONS - NO RESPECT

One of the benefits - or possibly side effects - of writing a gardening column is that it seems to come up a lot in conversation, sort of like a doctor who hears all about aches and pains, only they get paid. Last week I was visiting with my daughter-in-law's family, and talk quickly drifted to tulips and vegetables. I enjoyed the discussion, and they bought my dinner. What more could I ask?

Recently, I was at the dentist's office waiting for the hygienist to organize her tools. I couldn't take my eyes off the sickly plant in the corner. Actually, it was the only thing I could see other than the framed print on the wall. It was a spathyphylum, otherwise known as a Peace Lily, a typical graceful indoor plant. The leaves were unusually narrow, and uncharacteristically pointed upward, not drooping gracefully. Perhaps not enough light?

I tried to restrain myself, but lost the battle. "That plant looks like it's in trouble."

She said she knew that, but kept hoping it would recover. While I'm sure she couldn't overlook a tooth that was in trouble - more's the pity - she could easily ignore a plant which failed to cheer anyone in the chair. Probably a repotting and refreshed soil would do wonders for it, but she was, after all, busy. The comment was taken well, and led to a long discussion of gardening interests and stories. It served to take my mind off dentists, at least.

But the more memorable discussion this week was in the teacher's lounge at Licking Valley High School. I was a substitute that day.

"Hey - you write a gardening column. I can ask you!" I said I'd be happy to try to help.

"What's that ficus stuff they use at golf courses?"

"Ficus stuff?"

"Yeah, you know, that grassy stuff."

"Grassy stuff? You mean fescue?"

"Fescue? No, I think it's ficus."

Taking a stab, I said, "Ficus is a fig, like those fig trees you see in offices."

"Fig tree? You sure?" I wasn't.

Just then another teacher came in. "Hey, do you know what that ficus stuff is they use on golf courses?"

"Huh?"

"You know, ficus. That grassy stuff?

"I dunno."

Lost another couple of fans. They're probably still asking what that ficus stuff is. And I haven't a clue.

As for me, I've been planting, and doing what I've sagely advised you not to do. I rushed the seasons and planted some tomatoes and zucchini. I'm probably going to have to cover them on a cold night, but I'm willing to do that. Later, you will be safe in planting the warm weather plants, but you should keep an eye on the forecast and cover them if the temperature dips below 40 degrees, just to be safe.

Happy planting.

GARDEN TIPS I FIGURED OUT THE HARD WAY

In the years I've gardened, I've learned some important things (poison ivy has three leaves, hornets' nests are better left alone), and some unimportant things (indeterminate tomatoes get tall). I have also learned three things that are classic concepts that I will share with you today.

My first discovery was mulch. Years ago, I read about 80-year-old Ruth Stout's belief in mulching every spot of bare soil with spoiled hay. You can probably still find a book about her efforts. She lived on a farm. She claimed that mulch - the hay - conserved moisture, reduced weeds, kept the ground cool in summer and slowly added organic matter and nutrients to the soil, sort of a slow-release fertilizer.

She was right, and most gardeners now know it. I soon discovered the wisdom of her advice. She used any plant matter she could find as mulch. I tried her favorite - spoiled hay - in my vegetable garden and found it full of too many seeds and not very attractive. Next, I tried newspapers weighed down with rocks. It was pretty ugly, and the newspapers managed to get loose on windy days and blow around the yard.

You get the picture. Both of these things worked and were free or inexpensive, but nowadays I use nothing but shredded leaves in my vegetable garden, or hardwood mulch in the flower beds. These are both attractive and easy to come by.

Why do I go to all this work of spreading mulch once or twice a year? Several reasons. First, it's a lot easier than pulling weeds in the heat of July. I'm a lazy gardener and don't do things I can get away with not doing. But the main reason is the soil. When we moved here, we found hard-packed clay and sandstone, which became a mudslide in spring and brown concrete in summer. After just a few years of constant mulch, this clay became the black, fluffy stuff that gardeners dream about. It's so soft that I can put my hand completely in anywhere it has been mulched. (slight exaggeration)

The weeds are few because the seeds don't reach the soil. The ones that do make it through are usually spindly and easy to pull out with roots intact.

Mulch keeps my garden safe during both drought and torrential rains. It eliminates the need to turn the soil. The best soil is directly under the mulch, and turning it defeats the purpose. You probably won't believe this, but we haven't plowed or spaded our vegetable garden in years. We just add new mulch each year, and pull it back to plant.

Best of all, the hard brown color and the rich smell of the mulch makes me feel like a master gardener. Even though I'm not - yet.

My second discovery was edging the beds. Mulch works great when it's 2 to 4 inches thick, but at the edge of the bed the grass starts creeping in. An idle comment to my husband one day inspired him to cut a small trench around one. This formed an upright cut upward to the lawn on the outer edge, and sloped inward toward the bed on the other side of the cut. This gap discourages the grass and weed roots from crossing over. It looked professionally done instantly. My husband earned a job for life that day, which he grumbles about (but deep down he enjoys it.)

My third discovery catapulted me into greatness in landscape design - in my humble opinion. While we were edging the beds, we came to small place near the deck which held two trees and a pachysandra ground cover in a straight line on the outside edge. I suggested we curve out and back in to make it more interesting. Immediately we saw it was the right thing to do. It made us want to follow along the curving grassy path that resulted.

Since then, we have made all our beds with curving lines, and have reduced our weekly mowing time by one hour (less mowing, less trimming and no tight corners).

Each year, we add a bed of mulch somewhere. For example, we might put two or three trees into one bed with mulch, or create a bed along the house. We don't remove the grass - we just heavily mulch and edge the bed. As the mulch rots, the grass dies. This is my idea. I use lazy methods wherever possible, even if my husband is doing the work. I might need him to do some other job....

We let the mulch sit on the grass that way for one year, pulling out any grass or weeds that peek through, or throwing another scoop on thin spots all summer. The second year is much easier, as weed seeds have not been allowed access. Finally, we add plantings - shrubs, annuals, perennials, or ground covers, and edging.

Final tip: Mulching is a one-time job in the spring. Hoeing is a constant job and NEVER adds to the soil. I rest my case - mulching is King in my book.

GARDENING 'MISTEAKS' JUST HELP YOU LEARN

I wonder where the expression "green thumb" came from. The idea that some sort of magical touch is required to garden is ridiculous. Gardening is a science, not an art. At least not until you've gotten the basics down. While there are some artistic aspects in design, the rest is technology - and technology can be learned.

Don't get me wrong — there will be a lot of brown leaves between you and success, but everyone has those moments. Everyone. Even the experts. (At least I think.)

While I am not an expert, I have plenty of stories to tell to show that misteaks are everywhere. (oops - I hope the proofreader doesn't pull that one!) These are some humdingers:

One summer I planted lots of zucchini. My kids still run away when I mention that word, and they're in their 30's!

Another time I planted a real crabapple tree in my front yard. It looked terrible and the fruit was nasty.

I burnt everything with fertilizer - once.

This year in my greenhouse, I planted my flowering bulbs upside down in pots. All the leaves grew out around the edge, with the middle bare as Salt Flats. They were supposed to be Easter gifts for family members.

Once I planted mint around my patio. Took me 10 years to get rid of it. Ditto with Yucca.

I pruned the leader (main branch) of a tree, ruining its shape forever. I love to prune trees, but sometimes the branches are too thick to remove with a lopper (my large pruning shear). Once I left a 4" stub on a branch because it was narrow enough I could cut through it at that spot. In the emergency room later, my husband chastised me strongly as the doctor stitched up the gash on his head. I tried not to laugh.

We allowed our grapes to grow without pruning for 10 years. We got no grapes - just a terrific jungle to clean up.

More recently I planted perennials without labeling them. (I felt sure I'd remember). Then next year, I pulled them out thinking they were weeds. Expensive error.

My husband grumbled after I asked him to trim the main branch on the lilac bush because it was leaning backwards. As he cut it, it rolled halfway round and hit him on the head as it fell. He was complaining at the time. I had nothing to do with it.

I decided to mow our upper field one summer. It was 18" high, and the mower and I worked hard for two months to clear it. Not wanting to let it go back, I've kept it mowed since. I have visions of hydrangeas and azaleas covering it someday. That'll never happen.

As a present to me, my husband installed a small goldfish pond complete with a $14.95 Koi fish and some goldfish. The poor Koi had nowhere to hide in that small pond and a stray cat got him. I told my husband that even I don't get a $14.95 fish dinner! We soon got a larger pond and more Koi. No cat ever got another fish from us.

A month ago, I offered to "fix" my pastor's brown, straggly office fern. After major surgery, we now have two large and four small ferns, one of which I returned to the pastor while the others recuperate in my greenhouse. They're all green now, but still straggly, and the pastor is looking at me funny.

I could go on, but you get the drift. Mistakes are how we learn, in life and in gardening.

MAKING COMPOST AS EASY AS TAKING OUT THE TRASH

You probably think you need a degree in chemistry to make compost, or an expensive machine that guarantees compost in 14 days with just a flick of the wrist. Not true. Granted, my way takes a year or so, but it's easy.

"Why," you say, "should I bother?" Remember the dust Bowl of the 1930's? It was partially a result of using up the soil and not replenishing it. After that, savvy farmers realized that the land was their future and they should leave it better than they found it. I agree with that philosophy.

Compost does that, like a vitamin pill for your soil. It returns nutrients that are removed in the process of growing things. Like mulch, it's a non-burning, slow-release fertilizer and soil amendment. An important side benefit is that it reduces the over-crowding of our landfills, where yard waste never rots because it gets no air. Double benefit, right? A compost pile fits the bill for the ecologically minded. Besides, there's nothing as satisfying as the sweet-smelling, crumbly black earth of finished compost.

As for equipment, all you need is desire and a little space in your yard. A pile of garden trimmings behind a hedge somewhere doesn't require special tools. If you want to, you can turn it over occasionally with a garden fork, but you don't have to.

We have two piles: one we actively add to, and the other is the working pile. Working means it is slowly breaking down the contents, and this one does benefit from being turned occasionally with a garden fork.

Once I bought one of those plastic commercial composters, and it has long since cracked and been discarded. The open pile is still going strong.

What can go in it? Coffee grounds, potato peelings, egg shells, banana peels, spent flowers, dead house plants and potting soil, autumn leaves, dead house plants and soil, hedge trimmings - anything that once grew as plant material.

Does it smell? Not at all. Does it attract pests? Nope. (Don't add meat scraps or dairy items.) I add all my green kitchen wastes (coffee grounds, banana peels and even weeds) to the pile. One word of caution. Don't add any plant material that is diseased or insect-infested to the pile. Those should go in the trash.

The smaller you make these items, the quicker they will rot. We shred any leaves, cut up hedge trimmings, etc., so that they break down faster. And sometimes we don't. Depends on how tired we are.

You will want to keep some garden soil or leftover compost nearby to sprinkle on occasionally. The composted soil contains millions of microorganisms and speeds up the process like a red flag to a bull. You can also buy compost starter in the stores, but dirt is a lot cheaper. You could also use some compost from the first pile nearby with the same results.

The technical part of composting comes in the proper balance of greens grass clippings, kitchen wastes) to browns like leaves in fall (in green and brown layers). But at my house, the stuff goes on the pile when I have it - period.

You just collect the yard wastes and throw them into the pile. I collect kitchen waste in a lidded bucket under the sink. It's designed for that purpose. We use compostable plastic bags for lining the bucket. Hubby just carries the bag out and throws it on the pile. We empty the bucket frequently, because it fills often as you learn what makes compost. Keeping the compost pile accessible is a good idea so that trips there are easy. Another good idea is placing the pile in an out-of-the-way place. Neighbors appreciate that.

Because this is the slow way to compost, the pile doesn't heat up as much as the more labor-intensive method of frequent turning. So be patient. If everyone reading this article started a compost pile this year, think of the truckloads of space we would save in the landfills, and the tons of FREE "black magic" that would enrich our soil. You will enjoy the result of your efforts.

THINK IT OVER BEFORE PLANTING

What is the most important gardening activity? Planning! The average frost-free date in this area (Ohio) is May 15. Please note that that means half the time we have frost AFTER that date. You can call your local county Agriculture Extension office to find out your average frost-free date.

Good landscaping adds greatly to the value of your home and your appreciation of it. It's like washing your car - you enjoy it more when it looks good. If you would like to improve your landscape this year, here are some tips to consider as you plan.

Start by looking at what you have. Do you have enough shade? Color? Texture? Fragrance? Do you have plants standing by themselves all over the lawn so that mowing is a nightmare? Do shrubs block your view from the house, or wall you off from the street? Are walks and drives well-lit and unblocked?

Safety is a major factor if windows or porches are blocked so intruders can break in without being seen from the street, or can lie in wait for you behind overgrown plants.

It's amazing what a little elbow grease can do for shrubs and evergreens. Trimming back a plant will seldom harm it, and often makes a major difference in their appearance and in your ability to see safely. Read up on how to prune shrubs. Maybe I'll write an article on it.

Cleaning out untended portions of your lawn will make you and your plants feel better. Skip one of your workouts this week and apply those muscles to the home front. (This is an argument I frequently use with my husband. It doesn't work with him either.)

Work toward framing your view to the house. Trees shouldn't block the house. They should rise above it in back and on the sides, sort of like a picture frame. If you must plant trees in front for shade, choose large shade trees that can be pruned up high so the view is open when they are full-grown. Plant deciduous trees on the south side. Those are the ones that drop their leaves in the fall. They will block the hot sun in summer, and allow it through in winter after they lose their leaves.

Plant evergreens on the north or west sides (whichever brings the prevailing winds) to block the cold wind in winter. Plantings like these can reduce your heating and cooling expenses while they beautify your lawn.

Landscape architects talk about trees, understories and ground covers when they plan groups of plants. Understory plants are mid-size trees and shrubs that grow well near larger trees and fill in an isolated tree area beautifully. Dogwoods, redbuds, rhododendrons, and others are good choices, but your gardening center staff can give you some great ideas for your area.

Ground covers such as ivy, pachysandra, myrtle, hosta, and more offer a finishing touch. Do you see how a single tree can become a focal point of your lawn? Even better, it reduces the amount of lawn and is easier to mow around.

Don't be afraid to eliminate bad decisions from five years ago. A tree planted too closely to the house will never improve. Cut it down. A good gardener and a good photographer are not afraid to discard their mistakes. The difference is that a gardener can give away or move his/hers.

Before making a planting decision, think ahead 20 years. Don't plant a tree that will grow to 30 feet under the eaves of your house - or under the power lines. And my husband just reminded me to tell you not to plant balled Christmas trees that years later you will have to cut down. He calls them "dreaded pine trees". He once had to do that.

On the other hand, I've heard some people say, "I'm not going to plant trees. I won't be here long enough to enjoy them." Maybe you will. And if you aren't, someone else will enjoy the cleaner air and beauty. Trees add tremendous value to a home, and you will appreciate that when you sell the house. Planting a few around a new house is a great investment for the future. Large trees planted and located well add value to your property every year they grow. Consider it a gift to future owners and current neighbors - and to yourselves.

After attending to the "bones" of the landscape (the large plants, driveways, lighting, etc.), consider the smaller items. I try to add perennials every year, so I'll have a constantly fuller garden. I also use annuals every year for flowers and bloom.

Probably the best area to start on is the front entrance to your home. Is it inviting? Is it blocked or hidden by huge plants? Use low plants, flowers, interesting walkways, fragrant plants and good lighting to welcome your guests and call their attention to the entrance.

Like any other worthwhile job, improving your landscape can seem overwhelming at first. Starting is the hardest part, so pick out one area to work on this year - one. Then go talk to the local experts at the gardening center.

Don't get your plants at the grocery or hardware store. Get them where professionals can be found. They are paid to know horticulture, and to help you.

GARDENING LESSONS

One of the things I most like about gardening is the lessons it teaches me. I'm learning some tough ones this year. For example, you may remember I was worried about fertilizing our lawn, as we hadn't done it for a long time. I was afraid we would leave stripes with too heavy or too light an application. So we carefully applied the granules at half the recommended level one direction, and then went the other way with the other half. I needn't have worried. It was beautiful. So beautiful, in fact, that I decided to apply some Roundup to the few dandelions that were left. I carefully sprayed tiny amounts directly to the dandelions only, so the grass wouldn't be damaged.

Later when my daughter asked how she could help, I asked her to do the same thing. She, of course, sprayed some of the same dandelions.

Then came the rains. I was afraid they would rinse off Roundup, and they did, all over. Where we sprayed three inches, it spread to 12. About a week later, the grass began to turn brown in those spots. Worse, many spots ran together, so that entire patches are now completely bare. In between is beautiful soft grass laughing at us.

Our front lawn is pock-marked as if small bombs went off there. My son tells me it will probably take all summer to fill back in. He used to work at a local golf course as greenskeeper, and they had a tractor with a tank of Roundup that had a habit of dripping from the hose. He said everywhere he went with the rig, dead spots arrived a week later.

If my spotted lawn doesn't teach me humility, the English ivy bed certainly will. For some reason, this year has been particularly devastating to the ivy. It has struggled to survive, and everywhere I see beds of thin ivy and weeds. The weather has hurt it badly. I was so disgusted with mine that one day I simply ran through the outer three feet of the bed with the mower. Now I have a brown strip of ivy stems as a border. Not appealing.

As if to provide the final straw, tonight while mowing between showers, I looked up at our huge ironwood tree. I knew it was late in coming out, but it's worse than that. This tree has served as the primary sentinel to our driveway for more than 30 years, and now will have to be removed. What could be worse than losing a tree of over a total of 50 years?

Even in the midst of these discoveries, good things are happening, too. Our squirrel has found a walnut tree to raid, and now we have walnut and oak trees popping up everywhere. Last week, I potted two and Jim planted them on the hill. All this rain should give them a good start.

The plot I planted with heliotrope, moonflowers, and other annuals are filling in nicely, and I accidentally discovered a wonderful place to put them, under the pine tree by the log bench Jim made for me several years ago. The container accents the bench and makes the place seem cozier somehow. Even better, the shade will soften the stress on the plants inside.

But the best thing that happened recently is a spotted fawn curled up on on top of the hill last week. I held my breath as the mower crept closer and closer. She froze, too, hoping I'd pass by without noticing. Finally, she turned to look directly at me only three feet away, and then loped away the other direction.

I can be the best gardener possible and still not succeed. I can be the worst gardener possible, and still be blessed. It's not always up to the gardener. Nature holds the key. Learn to be patient during the bad times, and thankful when they're over. No wonder gardeners are nice people.

SOMETIMES PLANTS MUST BE PULLED

I'm feeling great today. Yesterday we worked in our flowerbeds for two hours, cleaning out over-grown and shaggy plants. Then we mulched those beds, and did it all before the sun was high in the sky. What a great workout. The benefits are visible today in the view from the window and as I park my car.

Gardening is a great workout. It involves strength training in lifting, digging, pulling and lugging bags of mulch. It involves aerobic exercise in walking to get all those tools I left behind in the garage and the last flowerbed. Finally, it involves bragging exercise in telling everybody about all the work you did today. That doesn't work with Jim anymore. He simply reminds me about the last time he was doing it while I was watching television. Ah, well.

So, you say, "Why on earth is a gardener pulling plants out?" Good question. I've confessed my habit of buying one plant at a time and sticking it in somewhere to see what happens. After living here for thirty years of this, it's beginning to show. Things are overgrown and difficult to weed and trim because of it. So, I have decided that less is more, and I am going to carry that out in my gardening plan. I like it best when things look neat and tailored, and they don't anymore.

Another reason I am removing plants is that they eventually get past their prime. Plants continue to grow as long as they are alive, and sometimes they lose their shape, their vigor, and their attractiveness. At that point, get rid of them. Trees are exempt from this because of their lengthy life span, but few other plants are.

Yesterday I removed some creeping thyme that is creeping all over my pond garden. Later I discovered thyme starting everywhere, and I'm sure I'll be fighting it for years.

I found some chives hidden in the middle of my irises. I took the chives out several years ago, after learning that they spread by seeds. I'm still pulling them out.

Next, I removed some irises near the pond because they haven't bloomed well for two years. I plan to remove some by my flagpole soon.

I took out some Thrift, a mossy creeping plant that was looking raggedy and loves to hide dandelions.

I removed withered tulip stems, and leftover annuals from last year. I know - I missed them then.

Finally, I removed the weeds that were easily visible afterwards. It's amazing how prominent a weed is when the bed is clean and mulched. That's another reason to keep it neat - it's lots easier to see the weeds and do something about them.

What's left, you say? A beautiful Japanese Maple, surrounded by three heathers, and nearby, a birds' nest spruce evergreen shrub and a burgundy perennial whose name I can't remember. After we mulched, it looked the way I remember it had when we originally installed it. Clean and neat.

I didn't have time to finish the whole bed, and the rest needs rehabilitation badly. I have three other beds to work on and mulch. An hour a day at this type of activity and both my body and my home will look a lot better. Since I can't beautify the whole county, I will start with just my little corner of it.

HAVING A POND REQUIRES CLEANING, LOVE AND PATIENCE

Yes, my friends, it's happening right here in River City (Licking County version). Pond fever has struck.

Barney and Janet Friel have collected a few victims of this virus. They've actually formed a group to discuss the effect and are calling it the Pond Club. The group recently held its first meeting at Barney and Janet's house, and future meetings will be held at various member's houses each month. The next program will be a landscaper talking, no doubt, about the use of water features in your garden.

While gardening is by definition working with plants, a water garden adds a whole new perspective of nature to your landscape. The attraction of frogs, fish, birds and sound can't be beat. Recently I discussed water gardens with a proud owner of one just installed last fall. When I told her that we had gotten lazy last spring and not cleaned the pond, and as a result lost many of our large Koi, her face fell.

"You have to clean it?"

"Well, yes," I replied, "but only once a year. You know, the leaves fall in and rot, and the plant material and other wastes ego to the bottom and need to be removed for the fish's survival during winter." (This from a person who just lost almost her entire quantity of fish.)

"Oh, we always scoop the leaves off right away."

I said nothing, because I don't. I surmised she had a big pond and further questioning proved it. She wasn't looking forward to cleaning it. I don't either, but I do look forward to the feeling I get when I see a spotlessly clean pool for the fish. They dart around the pond like new puppies.

I explained that it was only a matter of draining it, cleaning out the bottom, refilling it, adding one bucket of last year's water back to the clean water and waiting for it to return to normal temperature before returning the fish. (Note: I dip water from the pond into a wash tub, and then set about removing the fish to the tub until the cleaning process is over. If the sun is hot, or there isn't any shade, be careful to protect the tub from becoming too hot for the fish.)

She was far more concerned about her water turning green suddenly. "It's been beautifully clear, and all of a sudden it turned bright green."

"Well, it usually does that in the spring around the first sunny warm spell. It's called an algae bloom. It won't hurt anything and will gradually clear as the pond gets in balance."

"Balance?"

I could tell she was not happy about the way this conversation was going, and I wished we hadn't gotten into it.

The first year of having a pond is really a learning curve, I explained, and she would gradually learn about it. The thing is just to enjoy it, and watch and learn. As the plants grow each spring they begin to shade the pond and keep the algae from growing so much. The green growth on the pond liner is a healthy thing, I said, and she shouldn't worry about it. Actually, the algae in the water itself is normal too, but we pond owners avoid it because it's unattractive, and we can't see the fish.

Soon we moved on to the more pleasant aspects of owning a pond. My favorite is watching the frogs, which help keep the pond clean and free of insects. I was planning to order more tadpoles this year because they help to clean the pond's liner and was surprised to see we already had three or four tiny frogs born this spring. This is the first instance of hatching our own that I am aware of, and is probably a result of the unclean pond's layer of mud and leaves laying at the bottom of the pond all winter. This gave protection and a place for the eggs to hatch, possibly, even as it produced gases in the water that killed my favorite, Queenie. So my laziness helped the frogs and hurt the fish. Guilt crept in again. Queenie was the mother of many of the fish in the pond, and many bore her markings. She was the one who taught the little ones to come to the edge of the pond to be fed. She would eat pieces of food from my hand.

Sometimes I could touch her back as she fed. She was the only one I had named, and I miss her.

Now, though, I have about 10 or 15 one-inch fishes that I can watch grow their one inch per year. Many are interesting colors, and one is pure white. Albino? These are doing well in their newly cleaned home, and are learning that occasionally, food drops in and floats on top of the pond. I am tapping on a stone near the pond before I feed them. Someday I hope they will learn to come to the top just at the sound of the tapping, like Pavlov's dogs.

But the best thing I learned about our pond I learned from a young man who was looking at a ceramic frog at the edge of the pond. I was showing his mom around my little greenhouse 100 feet away. When it jumped about five feet into the water, he yelled, "HEY!" His mom looked at me worried. I said I think Seth found our frog. She laughed. It wasn't long before he learned that the frog would let him rub his back. I'll bet you folks without a pond have never done that, at least in your own back yard. When I told Jim about it, he immediately went out to the pond to try it himself. It worked......

VOLUNTEERING TO LEARN

How would you like to spend some quality one-on-one time with an expert garden designer, horticulturalist, propagationist, even a plant taxonomist, and pay no tuition for the privilege? I did recently when I spent a few peaceful hours at Dawes Arboretum as a volunteer.

My time began with Jennifer Ryan, who showed me some of her designs and photos. She is currently designing an herb garden for Daweswood, the home on the grounds. The garden is taking form already, lined with a low stone wall, and sits in full view of a beautiful pond, where the Canada geese shoosh to a stop on cool blue water. The garden will eventually hold a fountain and many herbs, currently being produced in the greenhouse. Paula McDonald, her two daughters and I, planted about 350 foxgloves around the house that day. I will enjoy going there again and seeing the foxgloves in full bloom. They are biennial (blooming two years).

Later, Jennifer showed me some of Dr. David Brandenburg's taxonomy files. These are neatly organized cabinets of sweet-smelling, carefully catalogued plants, glued and labeled on heavy paper. Some had a small envelope at the bottom, which Jennifer said contained seeds of the plants displayed. All were taken from the grounds of the Arboretum, and are an invaluable source of information. A huge press system was in use with new plants for his files, and I wondered what my sister-in-law would say about his press. She enjoys pressing flowers and making cards and wall hangings with them. While hers will accommodate a few flowers at a time, the Dawes' press was capable of doing many more. I wondered about the science behind carefully examining a plant for clues as to its identify, something like a plant private detective, I assumed.

Jennifer is also the volunteer coordinator for the Arboretum, and she introduced me to another volunteer who was working in the greenhouse that morning. She was helping to produce the plants that we were installing.

Jennifer showed me where she wanted the plants and explained why she was choosing those locations. She showed me maps of the grounds and took me on a short tour of the new composting program they are developing there. I saw the field of a new strain of apples found halfway around the world and discovered it to be a very hard, disease-resistant and tasty fruit. Dawes has taken the responsibility of growing the trees to maturity and working on developing them. Because trees have a very long development time, for obvious reasons, this is a process far too expensive and time-consuming for a nursery to attempt. As a not-for-profit organization, Dawes has agreed to use its considerable skills to develop this tree.

The next time I volunteered at Dawes, I spent my time with Rich Larson, a propagator. I was excited, as I love propagating plants. I found him happily checking on the many plants in his greenhouse. It looked like a mansion closed up in the owner's long absence, as there were clear and white plastic covers thrown over most of the benches. These, I later learned, were to protect the plants inside from too much light, or to contain the humidity even higher than that in the greenhouse. Individual trays were in a loose bag so that some air circulation would happen and prevent mold.

He was checking on the progress of cuttings and grafts. As he carefully inspected each plant for signs of growth, he sorted them into trays, those whose stock was healthy but the graft failed, and those headed for the compost pile because neither the stock nor the graft had succeeded. As we worked, I asked him many questions. He explained the grafting process. On healthy grafts, he pulled off the leaves on the stock and left the energy to go to the graft. Some plants he moved to the bench, uncovered, because he wanted them to get better light and to begin to harden off (be ready to plant). Others he kept under the bench until they were ready for the light. Some he put back under the plastic for even more protection. Others we moved to another tray and set them where they would be under the misting system.

The greenhouse was jammed with plants. One long bench held seedlings. I potted up some filbert trees, just six inches tall, from the seed tray to individual pots. I imagined someday gazing upward at them. Rich said if he had help like this every day, he could get a lot more done.

At this time of year (spring), greenhouse space was at a premium, as in most greenhouses. So was his time, and Jennifer's. A few more pairs of hands would make a vast difference in the work that they could accomplish. "You need more volunteers," I said. They agreed.

Volunteers could help with the herb garden, the all-season gardens planting annuals and perennials, raking, digging beds, mulching, sweeping, greenhouse planting and transplanting.

The pay is fresh air, a feeling of satisfaction, the ability to help a worthwhile cause, free exercise and knowledge you won't get in front of the TV. Perhaps knowledge you won't get anywhere else. (*Note: Dawes Arboretum is located outside Newark, Ohio, and is visited by people from vast distances.*)

WINDOW BOXES - CHARMING ADDITIONS TO HOME

If you have adult children, you can probably relate to this story. A year or so ago, my husband made two window boxes for our son and daughter-in-law. They have a Cape cod style house, nestled among huge trees near Cleveland. They wanted some old-fashioned window boxes, so Jim made them a pair for Christmas. Dan said he wasn't sure how to attach them, but he could probably get someone to do it for him. (hint, hint) He painted them and stored them in the garage, where they still are. This spring, Jim got some brackets made to attach them to the house, and we are going up to do that. More accurately, Jim and Dan will do it.

It occurred to me that, past experience taken into account, they will probably want some advice as to what to put in the boxes. (My daughter-in-law has an exceptional ability to make us feel important by asking our advice. Dan chose well.)

First, window boxes must have plenty of drains to prevent water logging, and I made sure that Jim bored several holes in the bottom of each one. A friend of mine had two plastic window boxes, and she asked me why one kept falling off the window ledge and the other didn't. A little inspection showed why: one had drain holes and the other didn't.

When the one filled with water, it slid off the ledge, as well as drowned all the plants. Drainage done, your window box will be much drier than the ground, because it is not surrounded by cool moist soil as the plant would be in the ground. If you are a better waterer than I am, your plants will not suffer for this.

Knowing my daughter-in-law, who once said, "You have to WATER houseplants?", I think I will recommend plants for her boxes that will withstand drought. Lots of it. Very tough plants. But beautiful. Maybe plastic?

Just kidding about plastic. I guess we can hope that rain will occasionally reach the boxes.

Second, we will want some color that complements the house colors. Theirs is tan with white trim and a deep plum or burgundy-colored front door. So good colors would be blue, lavender, white, mauve, and of course, green.

My daughter-in-law is better at this than I am, and more creative, so I will rely on her tastes here.

Third, window boxes need some plants for height, some for middle level, and some that will drape over the edge and hang down. Different textures can add greatly as well.

For example, a spiky plant or tall flowering plants would add height. Geraniums might be a good choice for color and drought resistance, though I don't know of any blue or lavender ones. White is certainly available, and blue could be added other ways. For early spring, pansies withstand frost well, so could even be planted now, and many blue or lavender varieties are available. These, however, are not tall, so height might have to wait until May. Pansies could be crowded in so that they hang over the front edge slightly. Their cheery blooms can really brighten a dull wintry day.

For next year, perhaps in the fall, some daffodils could be planted in the boxes (these are plenty deep), and those plus pansies would be an eye-popping blue and yellow combination, with height and texture the following spring.

One plant that drops over the edge of the box and is fairly hardy as far as drought is concerned, is the vinca vine. These are light green with white edges, and tend to run in straight lines downward, so they have a neat draping appearance. They are very attractive with geraniums, for example.

The best way to choose plants is to take these recommendations and your color choices to the nursery and ask the experts there for advice about color, height, and texture combinations. They put these things together every day and have excellent advice.

I can't wait to take the first photographs of their house with the new window boxes mounted and filled with beautiful plants.

AROMATHERAPY AND DEAD FISH: IRONY OF GARDENING

I hope you're rushing the season this year by forcing some blooms in your own living room. "What," you say, "is that?"

Forcing branches is a fancy term for bringing some shrub twigs inside, placing them in a large vase with water, and waiting for the surprise. If you have a Forsythia bush, a pussy willow, even fruit trees or flowing trees, and they usually bloom in spring, you may be able to enjoy their blossoms a little longer by using this method. This is my means of aromatherapy, at least for this time of year. What better time to do this than after a long winter to appreciate Mother Nature's gifts to us?

Even though we've been blessed by a gentle winter, I'm ready for some greenery and those fragrant blossoms. You can actually prolong the effect by making cuttings every few days and bringing them in. Realize, though, that in the case of fruit trees, you are removing potential fruit-bearing branches. If the tree or shrub is large, you probably won't miss them, but if not, better look elsewhere for your living room blooms.

I had a call this morning from a neighbor who is concerned that he is gradually losing goldfish in his pond this winter. He wondered if I had noticed this. I haven't. One year, I lost all but one of my fish, but it was because I had gotten lazy the spring before and hadn't cleaned the pond. Apparently, there was too much debris in the bottom for them to survive the winter. Leaves and other debris as they decay emit a gas that is poisonous to fish, especially if the pond is covered with ice. For that reason, it is important to keep a hole in the ice to let in oxygen and let out the gas. I use a stock tank de-icer to maintain a small hole all winter long. It is electrical and floats on top of the water, keeping a hole about double the size of the de-icer.

He said he had cleaned the pond last year. I asked about lawn chemicals that might have seeped into the pond, but he said they didn't use any. After thinking about it, I realized that if that were the case, the fish would probably have all died at the same time. He said he had seen the fish eat ladybugs and spit them out occasionally. It could be a pond disease, I suppose. But I haven't had to deal with any of those.

Today I have made myself a promise to plant some lettuce in the garden and some flowers in the greenhouse.

I have delayed too long. Busy schedules can keep us from the things we love, and that makes us no good to anyone.

If you are a gardener, find some dirt today to dig in. It'll revive your soul.

ENJOY PLANNING, DOING, AND REMEMBERING

Sunny days and propagation mats have cooperated in germinating many of the seeds we planted two weeks ago. First to come up were basil, then broccoli. After that, most of the rest came up simultaneously. Broccoli, red petunias (but not blue), lobelia, blue fescue ornamental grass, one lonely tomato, moonflowers, and morning glories all have sprouted and are reaching for the sun. After they showed above the soil, I moved them to a cool bench to make more room on the propagation mat, and watered them very gently with the mister.

I noticed this week that I'm not the only one running up the hill to check on the plants. Both Jim and Mandi regularly report how things are going, and sometimes ask me accusingly, "Have you checked on the garden today?" Jim is particularly cocky this week, as someone asked me last Sunday if I ever gave him a day off. I said no. Why should he be any different than me? Anyway, he's been smiling ever since.

As the red petunias germinate, I am thinning them daily. The first day, I reduced the number of plants per pot to two or three, depending on the size of the full-grown plant, and each day I go through the process again. I learned to plant plenty in each pot, in order to save on potting soil, time, and bench space. Not all seeds germinate, and that eliminates the wasted pot syndrome which I had at first by planting one seed in a pot. Now, with at least two, I can always transplant one of the extras to a pot that for some reason doesn't germinate at all, or discard them as necessary. I usually wait until the first two leaves have formed before I do the thinning. I still plant more than I need so I can give away the extras. This gives me more enjoyment than growing the produce in my own garden.

I tried a new heirloom tomato this year, called Druzba. I think the name attracted me, and I love the taste of heirlooms. I learned, though, that the look of heirlooms can be a turnoff, even if the taste is sensational, so I have tried to stick to ones that at least look red or pink and have a round shape. One exception that I have used every year is the rainbow heirloom, a yellow variety with beautiful red streaks in the center. It is a very attractive tomato, especially when sliced on a plate or a sandwich, and the taste is out of this world. Until you taste a hybrid variety and an heirloom variety side by side, you won't understand the difference. Only one plant has germinated so far, so I am wondering if it is a different variety than the rest, or else the germination rate is exceedingly low. I hope not.

The one plant that I am excited about having again this year is the Blue Fescue ornamental grass. I planted many seeds in each small pot, and intend to use it almost as a plug. Several years ago, I planted some of this, and it eventually grew into beautiful small clumps of grass that came back year after year in tightly bunched grasses with excellent blue color that contrasts nicely with other greens. Because

I had to replace some plants eventually, and they no longer looked uniform in size and texture, I eventually removed all of them and gave them away. This year, I can look forward to having another series of grasses as a border.

As a friend of mine used to say about her trips, I enjoy my garden in the planning, the doing, and the remembering.

MOTHER NATURE SPEAKS

It's not even the end of tax season yet, and I've already experienced my first gardening failure. Jim informed me that our three tiny cabbage plants now look like wilted lettuce. Apparently, the frost was more a freeze, and they weren't up to it. So, we'll have to start those again, whenever I get around to it. Both they and Jim are saying, "I told you so!"

My pansies laughed at the freeze, or maybe they are in a more protected place. I am enjoying their bright blue color as I pass by every day. On the opposite side of the drive is the large container I planted last year and enjoyed so much. I left it out all winter so I would have some structure to look at, but now it's calling to me, saying, "Plant me, please." It would be a great time to refresh it and leave it in the greenhouse for another six weeks or so. I'll put that on my to-do list.

Did you know that plants talk to gardeners? You just have to know their language. Even weeds do too, but usually they are saying, "Stop procrastinating, and pull me out of here before I run wild." Sometimes these comments are so distracting, it's difficult to have a conversation with a friend who's touring the garden with me.

The greenhouse is on its second batch of plants. The first have all germinated, been thinned and moved to hardening-off benches, so the mats are free to warm the toes of another set of seed flats. These include Rainbow tomatoes (my favorite), alyssum, and mixed Columbine. Columbine is a perennial, but a tall one, so I'm not sure where I'll put them.

As for the vegetable garden, Jim's domain, we have added some radishes, spinach carrots, beets and peas in the last couple of weeks. Hopefully, we won't have any more hard freezes, and we can safely move into the cool growing season. The broccoli in the greenhouse is still not sturdy enough to move outdoors, so I'll wait through the best part of the season. I started those too late. Life intervened, I guess. At least that's my excuse. I've never had a seed talk to me like a plant.

As soon as the ground warms up, the next and biggest task of the year is mulching the beds. I enjoy doing this, as it looks so beautiful when we're finished, and it smells so clean. It's good exercise, too, but I still put it off some years. I have learned that if I don't do it early, I lose the urge. If we mulch too soon, it slows down the warming of the soil, and that slows down the plants and everything else that goes into the beds. So early May is probably a good time, providing it's not too cold.

Last night I opened the back door to let the dog out and heard a pleasant sound. I had forgotten that Jim had cleaned the leaves from the top of the pond and re-installed the filter and pump. It was such a pleasant gurgling sound that

I wanted to go out and relax awhile to listen. The birds told me they enjoyed it, too, and then got ready for the night. It was too chilly, so I didn't, but I will soon. I always do what Mother Nature says to do - almost.

DREAMING OF SPRING

I just completed my third trip of the spring to the local nursery, and came back with a trunk full of plants, all blooming or about to do so. There's nothing like inhaling the sweet perfume and color of flowers after a long, cold winter to bring up your visions of warm summer breezes and iced tea on the deck. I didn't realize that was what I was looking for until I reached the checkout lane. There, I saw that every plant I chose had blooms. Later, it will be the cool colors of green that will catch my eye, but not now.

I came home with a beautiful red flowering quince, a flat of blue pansies, a couple of yellow and red dahlia bulbs, three red Bergera daisies, one pale yellow hibiscus, a white Hellebores, and a very tall and on sale acer rubrum "Red Sunset", or red Maple. The dahlias will wait until May to go in the ground, and the Hibiscus even later, but they will make a striking group with the daisies once the weather becomes trustworthy again. I have tried planting hellebores two or three times before and never succeeded. This time, I purchased a two-gallon pot with a well-rooted shrub. Hopefully, I'll be able to report a success by this time next year. It is a plant that blooms in the winter and early spring, and is semi-evergreen, I think. It thrives in full or partial shade, and the flower is reminiscent - at least to me - of the dogwood. If it doesn't go this year, I will try no more. (Yes, it blooms in the winter.)

Dahlias are a reliable flower with lots of blooms, if you are willing to dig them up in the fall. The bulbs won't last through the winter. If you'd rather not dig them up, you can consider them an annual, leave them in the ground and buy new ones the following year. There are so many types to choose from, all beautiful, that it's hard to imagine they are all dahlias. Try a couple; you'll be pleasantly surprised. Wait until the danger of frost is past before planting - probably mid-May. At the end of the blooming season, in September or so, you can dig them up and have another pleasant surprise: they multiply, so you'll be blessed with more bulbs. Give them to your friends, or just have a more massive display the following year.

Henry Mitchell once said, "There is nothing like the first hot days of spring when the gardener stops wondering if it's too soon to plant the dahlias and starts wondering if it's too late." Now is too soon.

The red maple, so named for its gorgeous fall display, has tiny dark red leaves opening now. I will have to choose a site carefully for this beauty, because I have a feeling I'll be standing at the window often to admire it. During the summer, it's green, but in the early fall it turns a bright scarlet that gives it the "red sunset" variety name. I will be setting out the post-hole diggers before Jim comes home.

I realize I'm no fish-and-game columnist, but have any of you noticed the wild turkeys that are about? I have lived my whole life in Ohio, and never saw a wild turkey until a month ago. In the last four weeks, I have seen four different pairs of turkeys on country roads. These were in four different locations, and all were perusing the grassy areas near the road. When the car passed, they leaned forward and ran away. They are fascinating to watch as they run. They are easy to recognize, though they are much thinner, sleeker, and healthier looking than the ones we have bred for domestication and Thanksgiving dinners. Those, you may remember, are so dumb that the hens lay their eggs standing up, so that the eggs break when they hit the ground. I have a feeling that the wild varieties don't do that.

Anyway, kudos to our game management people for this amazing success of a species that had all but disappeared in our neck of the woods.

There's an old Chinese proverb that says, "If you wish to be happy for a day, get drunk. If you wish to be happy for a week, kill a pig. If you wish to be happy for a month, get married. If you wish to be happy forever, make a garden." Don't get mad at me. I didn't write it.

DIVIDING PERENNIALS BENEFICIAL, FRUGAL

"Can I divide my peonies now?"

"I'd like to move my hostas. Is it safe to do it in spring?"

Think about it. Springtime is when everything else is multiplying. Why not hostas and peonies?

Division is a form of propagating perennials vegetatively - that means without seeds. The price? Free. For many perennials, division is the best way. Now, when they are just breaking ground and you can see exactly where they are, is a great time to dig them up and split them.

Peonies and hostas are typical examples of vegetative (non-woody) perennials that respond well to division. Bulbs, of course, also like to be divided, as do ferns, ornamental grasses, ground covers and many other plants. (Caution: Bamboo is a rampant spreader. Not something for the yard or any place, in my opinion.) Gardeners also respond well to this process, as bragging rights abound. "Didn't cost me a thing," they say.

How do you do this? Mostly with elbow grease. Let's say you have a large clump of a perennial, and you've noticed it looking less brilliant than in previous years. I usually get out my English spade for this job. That's a square-tined short-handled fork that's very effective and easy to use to dig up plants and loosen the soil. You can also use a shovel, or hand any of these to your spouse. That's what I usually do. Back to planting: you then take small clumps of the original and spread them out. Remember the size of the first clump, and space accordingly.

So, after digging you have a bucket-sized clump of soil, roots and plants. Lay it on a few sheets of newspaper and study it for a minute. I usually divide a clump this size into quarters. If you're strong and the clump isn't, a shovel can work. I have also used a large knife, though not for long, or an axe. Whatever works for you. Just be careful.

Once the root ball is quartered, simply plant each quarter in a new spot, plant them in a row, or give some away. Now there are four plants where once there was one. "But," you say, "that plant just got to a nice size. why would I want to mutilate it like that?" Perennials actually prefer to be divided every two to three years, and often respond with a burst of growth or bloom.

For example, my daffodils this year are producing lots of leaves but few blossoms. It's time to dig them up and spread them out. Can I do it now? Yes, and it's probably best while I'm thinking of it. Best for me - not necessarily for the plant. But they will survive it.

A couple of years ago, I helped my son and daughter-in-law pick out some plants for their lawn. One was liriope (pronounced ler-AYE-oh-pea), a nice ornamental grass with attractive blue flowers. We didn't have enough to finish lining the edge of the flower bed, and when we went back to the nursery, they were sold out. The following spring, I suggested to my son that he try division. His eyes lit up. He's a tightwad businessman. I don't know where he gets it. I told him to divide them in halves, since they were only a year old. But he went into fourths and had enough to finish the whole job. It will just take them a little longer to reach full size. At the price we paid for the originals, $7.99 each, he saved approximately $96 plus tax. Better yet, he was sure they would all match.

It was almost enough to make him a gardener.

A HORTICULTURIST'S WORK IS NEVER DONE

We finally got a break in the rain at the same time that we were both home long enough to mow the grass. It was embarrassingly high. By the sound of the lawn mowers up and down the road, we weren't the only ones catching up on our duties. We have contracted with a company to fertilize and weed treat our lawn three times a year, and the result is that the lawn grows very fast, especially in the spring. Later on, it slows down, but right now, it seems to grow inches after every rain and we've had a lot of those.

The good news is that the dandelions and other weeds are beginning to disappear. Even the ground ivy is less prevalent. Apparently, it's difficult to get rid of because its waxy coating on the leaves tends to repel the chemicals. Smart weed. But the healthy grass is crowding it out somewhat. With a heavily treed lot as ours is, the shade and tree roots are tough competition for grass, so a fertilizer helps considerably. The worst spots in our front yard are the ones where I decided last year to use RoundUp on the dandelions, thinking I could be careful not to get it on the grass. The dead spots got larger as the summer progressed, and are still there this year. I won't make that mistake again. It says on the bottle, "Not recommended for lawn weeds as it may kill the grass as well." I never was very good with directions. And with recent warnings about cancer-causing RoundUp, I wouldn't recommend it anymore at all.

As we mowed, I noticed that our friends the ground moles have started their annual polka-dotting of the lawn. We've tried many things and found nothing that works for long. The best thing was a Black Snake that took up residence in our front lawn a couple of years ago. The second best was one of our cats that seemed to enjoy grabbing these little guys. Third best was a non-poisonous powder that controls the reproduction of the grub worms that moles supposedly like - milky spore, it was called. I guess I've resigned myself to the fact that they are going to win.

After the break in the rain allowed us to cut the grass, I was able to corral Jim to help trim the evergreens on the hill.

I'd done the ones nearer our house for two years and had seen a measurable improvement in thickness and shape, but hadn't made it up to the hilltop yet. So we trekked up with pruners and small saws, tractor and trailer, and trimmed the smallest evergreens. Several had deer damage, and probably won't do well, but we pruned anyway to see what happens by next year. He is a quick learner, so it went easily. We imagined a cone shape and cut everything away that stuck out beyond that. Except, of course, the main trunk, which we left to its own devices. Anyplace where the tree is thin, we were especially careful to nip the ends out as well, even though we wanted to leave every needle to fill the gap. Trimming the ends tends to thicken the branches, and we really needed thickness in the sparse areas.

While we were there, we also limbed up (cut a few of the lower branches off) a number of small trees that have been growing without much attention for two or three years. These looked much better afterwards, and now resemble a healthy tree rather than a shaggy bush. We never removed more than one-third of the foliage, as that would be a major shock to the tree and could even kill it eventually. There's always next year to take more off.

Then there were the dogwoods. What a sad thing to see these gradually declining every year. New ones continue to spring up, though, and I've heard rumors that they are beginning to develop an immunity to the anthracnose that is affecting them. I hope it's true. The only other option is to plant the Korean variety, which is supposed to be resistant. I may resort to that if this continues. No trimming is necessary on these beauties, but some had broken and dead branches falling around from the winter winds, and these had to be pulled down to the burn pile. Who needs a membership at the health club when you have inspiring work like this in a beautiful setting? (I do.)

While I developed a HUGE blister on my thumb from pruning, Jim worked happily away without complaint. I wonder what he's up to?

POND MAINTENANCE: REWARDS WELL WORTH THE WORK

As the days get warmer, I know it's time to clean the pond. I already have some babies in mine, according to my daughter.

The filter has been running for a couple of weeks, and the water is not getting any clearer. It probably won't, as the pond has a year's worth of rotting leaves, leftover fish food and fish waste at the bottom, and even a filter won't handle those. Our process is usually to clean the pond in the spring, once a year, and do it by clearing it of leaves as we see them, not over-feeding the fish, and not loading the pond with too many fish.

"That sounds like work," you say.

It's much less work than maintaining the same area of grass or other plantings. No weeding or weekly mowing. Besides, it's year-round entertainment. Even in the winter, I am often called out to shiver by the pond to see how the fish are doing. On a warm January day, sometimes the fish come up from their hibernating spot below to swim sleepily around the top of the pond, probably to get some fresh air.

The frogs are already active, and very early this year. Jim found Missy, our black Lab, sniffing at something on the patio next to the pond. It turned out to be a large frog, who was really happy when Jim got Missy's attention long enough for him to do his hopping thing out of there.

When Jim took out the stock tank de-icer, and replaced it with the biological filter in early March, he said the pond was loaded with snails. Years ago, I began buying a few snails and tadpoles every year from a mail order pond supply house. It was great fun watching the tadpoles grow up, sprouting legs along with a tail, and then changing into little frogs. The little ones become big ones by the end of the season. Around September or so, they seem to disappear from the pond, or maybe to hibernate below, but they come back in the spring.

When we first got the pond, we cleaned it in the fall, concerned about the falling leaves that were collecting there, despite our attempts to keep the top skimmed clean. We knew that rotting leaves produce a gas harmful to fish and animals, especially if trapped under a layer of ice. But we found that the frogs and snails had to be replaced every year. Later, I read that they needed a layer of mud in the bottom to hibernate under for protection during the winter. Once we switched our cleaning regiment to spring, the frogs and snails thrived. This is the earliest we have seen frogs since we started a pond about six years ago. That may be the result of a very mild winter, or of good management. I prefer good management.

So how do we clean the pond? We detach the pump hose from the fountain and place it in a large bucket next to the pond and simply begin pumping out the water. We remove the plants while the pump works, and set them in a bucket of pond water. Some of the water we dump into a large galvanized tub to hold the fish as we find them. We watch for fish and catch them as gently as possible in a fish net and place them in the tub. The tiny ones often glitter in the sunlight, but they are difficult to catch. We leave the pump in a plastic dish pan so that it doesn't start sucking in mud as we get to the bottom. The process of pumping takes an hour or two, and we quickly run out of space in the tub for water. The rest we carry to the flower beds as fertilizer. We don't put it on the vegetable garden for fear of contamination, but the flowers love it.

As we get to the bottom, we carefully search the muck and leaves for fish, frogs, or snails. There's not much danger of keeping a frog in a pile of muck for long, though. They usually take matters into their own feet. We usually have some black fish in the mix, which we discard or "cull", because you can't see them in the pond. That is one way to keep the population down and maintain the color we want.

Once most of the water is out, we (Jim) climbs into the pond and cleans it thoroughly by rinsing and dipping a couple of times. We never clean off the green growth on the sides of the pond, as this is a healthy growth that helps keep the water clean and the fish fed.

While we are cleaning, we're careful to put some plants in the tub to give the fish some shade and some hiding places, and if we leave them in the tub overnight, we cover the tub with some netting. In the tub, they are sitting ducks for a stray cat or coon that comes along. I once fed a stray cat a $14.95 fish dinner with my new Koi this way.

Once the pond is clean, we begin to fill with clean water. Since the water is much colder than the previous temperature of the water, I add some hot water I heat on the stove. I test repeatedly to closely match the temperature of the water in the tub. A sudden temperature change will kill the fish quickly. Once the pond is full and the temperature is adequate, we begin to net the fish in the tub and replace them in the pond. They always respond gratefully - darting around the pool like a teenager in a new convertible. The final step is to add one bucket of water from the tub into the pond. Yup - the dirty water. It contains thousands of microorganisms that will quickly rebound in the pond to make it a healthy environment for the fish. We don't fill it completely at first, because as the pond adjusts temperature, it is safer to add small amounts of cold water at a time to fill it. The next day or two I add small amounts of water, as needed.

One more thing - don't be surprised if the water turns bright green in a week or two. This is a natural part of the process that will quickly reverse itself. Just keep that filter running, and you'll be pleased with the result.

If you'd like to learn more about managing your pond, do some research about local ponds clubs for help. Call the local County Extension office for information.

PEACEFUL MOMENT PRUNING SHEARS AND GENTLE RAIN

This morning, I awoke early, and went out to the deck to listen and watch the sun rise. I took a book, a jacket and a cup of coffee. What a great way to start the day. The birds sang, Missy enjoyed snuffling around for spiders and frogs, and I relaxed as I hadn't in days. Jim came out with his breakfast, and we sat together for a while. Soon a gentle rain began to fall as the sun came up. There's nothing I enjoy more than sitting under cover and watching it rain. Jim smiled and went in to get ready for work.

My redbud tree is in full bloom in front of the rail fence. A fat grumpy robin sat on the fence with his feathers fluffed, watching me. Behind the fence a white dogwood contrasted with the purple redbud. I wished I had a camera.

Soon my eye was drawn to the evergreens planted up the hill a way. They looked much thicker than last year, but still had some sparse areas. A couple were showing some deer damage, as if they had been nibbled from the top down. Now they're shaped like a child's pedal car, low and wide. I wondered if they could be rehabilitated. I doubted it, but made a mental note to try. Soon my coffee cup was empty, and as I went inside to refuel, I grabbed my trusty holster belt with my Felco pruners and gardener's Leatherman tool also holstered nearby. I buckled up and brought the coffee along. I always feel important when I buckle this rig on.

As It rained very softly, I approached the first pine tree. It was about 4 feet tall, and shaped fairly well. I snipped idly at the main branches, just shortening each one about an inch from the tip. Several branches showed a drying tip where I had trimmed them last year. The branches there were filling in toward the center, so it was working. As I moved to the rear of the tree, however, the branches were few. A row of trees at the fence line shades this side, and any branches there were thin and reaching for the light. I snipped every one of these, hoping for some fill in the back. Though it seems to be contrary to logic, tip pruning usually results in the strength of the plant moving to the side shoots on the branch rather than toward the end, making for a much thicker and sturdier plant.

Every snip brought a strong scent of pine, and I enjoyed the work. Later, I cleared out the center and suckers from the bottom of a small dogwood tree that looked a little cluttered in the view from my new kitchen window. Several vines attached to the tree with many little fingers and got snipped everywhere I could get my pruners underneath. This was poison ivy, and I was careful not to touch it or the blades on my pruners after that.

The rain grew heavier, but I ignored it. I love the rain. I was in a groove, and didn't want to stop. I pictured thick, perfectly shaped trees as I worked. I moved to others, one of which was a three-foot blue spruce. This one produced a new scent when cut, and I tried to remember it for the future. Several of the smaller trees had almost a flying saucer shape toward the top of the tree, and these I shortened more than one inch. I tried to attain a conical shape to the tree, while also coaxing more strength into certain weaker branches. But I never cut the leaders, the main trunk, of a tree. It will stunt the growth permanently.

I angled the next ring down from the leader in toward the main stem, about six inches lower than the leader's top height. I saw that done in a Christmas tree nursery, and the trees there were plump and perfectly shaped, except for the leader, which rose a few inches taller than the rest. I figured they must know what they're doing, so I copied this technique.

One of the blue spruces had several dried or dead branches, as if damaged by deer or pests, though I saw no definite proof of either.

Soon the rain came down harder, and a brief flash of lightning, but I still worked on. Not far behind were a bright flash and a big boom. I headed for the house - fast. I made a mental note to also shape the two arborvitae near the house, and to try to propagate those in the greenhouse.

Yup. An excellent start to the day.

EMOTIONS RUN HIGH ON WINDOW BOXES

I spent a couple of hours yesterday thinking about window boxes. My husband made some for our beautiful daughter-in-law, and yesterday we delivered them to Cleveland. While Jim and Dan collaborated over how to mount them to the house, Annette and I went to the very busy nursery nearby. My advice to her was to decide on a color scheme, then try for three heights in the box: tall, medium, and trailing over the edge. The rest was up to her.

Their house is tan and white, with a deep rusty-red front door, so we debated over the color scheme. She said that Dan wanted some really bright color like red and white. She had a picture from a magazine of two window boxes in full sun that had struck her fancy. They were very full of plump healthy vines and mid-height flowers like petunias. Her boxes are in what I would call deep to mottled shade - pretty heavy stuff. So we asked for help at the door as we went in. The gentleman said red was a little hard to come by in shade, except for perhaps begonias.

She wasn't too thrilled with the begonias, as they were full-leaved and a little disheveled-looking. I guess there's no accounting for tastes. We picked out some New Guinea Impatiens, then learned they were partial sun, and gave up on them. We found an attractive new Vinca vine with green and chartreuse leaves, and she liked those, but we couldn't find enough of them to do the job. Back to the drawing board.

We saw some vines in the back and headed that way. On the way I noticed some Helichrysum - a silver gray fuzzy vine that fills a lot of container gardens - and I called her attention to it. That she liked, and there were plenty.

Eventually, we picked out red impatiens (that was her idea from the beginning), a plant with small white flowers and dark green leaves and the helichrysum. Homage to the Buckeyes. We bought the potting soil, some perlite to lighten the weight of the soil and the box, and asked for some of the soil crystals that hold moisture so that plants require less watering. We found a huge container that cost $34, so passed on that.

We rushed back home to find the men folk starving (they apparently don't know how to turn on the stove) and headed for a restaurant (we apparently don't either). Gardeners need nourishment just like the plants. After a relaxing lunch, we headed back for the fun part.

We bought too many plants, it seemed. They looked so small on that huge bench. In the flower boxes, we dumped a mixture of potting soil and perlite and spread it out about half as deep as the box. Then we set the plants in, pots and all, for a test of how they'd look when planted. They looked okay, so we began to remove the pots and reset the plants minus pots. The next step was to gently fill potting soil around the plants, taking care to keep the tops level with the soil, and firming gently as we went. The final step was to water it all thoroughly.

My daughter-in-law wanted to be sure that the boxes held lots of red, since that was what her husband wanted. Wouldn't you know that the bedding plants, the Impatiens, were almost hidden from view behind the larger, potted, other plants? She looked very uneasy, but I assured her that soon those Impatiens would be dominating those window boxes.

If they don't, I think I'll stay on this side of the state for a while.

HEIRLOOM TOMATOES YIELD TASTY MEMORIES

The average frost-free date in this area (Central Ohio) is May 15. That means HALF of the time you can still expect frost before that date. If you hear the forecast for frost, you cover the plants for protection. (An old sheet, maybe?) You can plant your warm weather crops like tomatoes after that date. The odds are that you'll be covering them up a couple of times to protect them from frost, but real gardeners don't mind. It keeps you in touch with nature, or at least in touch with newspapers, boxes and bed sheets.

I am excited about one of my crops this year: Heirloom tomatoes. Some define these as tomatoes that have been around for at least 50 years, and handed down in families or communities. That means they are NOT hybrids, so their seeds can be saved for next year.

Hybrids are a cross between two varieties of plants and produce fruit that is different from both parents. You could get a real strange plant, in other words, if you used seeds from hybrids.

Many of our common tomato hybrids have been developed for the commercial tomato industry, which means they have to have tough skins and ripen off the vine to withstand long shipping and sitting on grocery aisles, be disease resistant, and look perfect. Taste is less important in this case.

But if you can walk out your back door to pick a tomato for your sandwich, taste is the biggest consideration.

Why do heirlooms taste better? I have read that it's because they are indeterminate (vine type). That is, they keep growing until frost. This gives more leaf for each fruit, and therefore, more flavor than the determinate, or bush, varieties. For this reason, make sure you stake them.

My friend Gary and I collaborated on our tomato plants this year. (Gary is the reason I have a greenhouse. He built an inexpensive one and shared the plans with us!)

He started three varieties of heirlooms for me, and I started two for him. Gary plans to grow many heirlooms this year. He has set aside a special pot for one of each variety, and plants to keep notes on production and flavor of each type. This level of organization is scary for me, but it works for him.

This year I'll be trying Red Brandywine, Pink Brandywine, Rainbow, Delicious, and Mortgage Lifter.

Like that last name? A man known as Radiator Charlie repeatedly crossed four of the largest tomatoes he could find. When he got one he was happy with, he sold transplants for a dollar apiece, and in six years paid off his mortgage. Hence the name, Radiator Charlie's Mortgage Lifter.

Another man, Craig LeHoullier, got a letter and some tomato seeds from J.D. Greene of Sevierville, Tenn. The "purple" tomato had been in a neighbor's family for years. LeHoullier was delighted to find a true purple tomato that was delicious as well. This tomato became known as Cherokee Purple.

I can't guarantee a paid-up mortgage for you, but I can guarantee you'll have a conversation piece with heirlooms, and I hope you'll have a good tomato on your sandwich. You can learn more about heirlooms by searching on the internet under "heirloom tomato seeds".

If you want to save the seeds from your heirlooms, scoop out the seeds and pulp from a ripe tomato, and spread them on several thicknesses of paper towels or newspaper. Let them dry thoroughly, and store in an airtight container, well-marked with the year and variety. Gary keeps his in old prescription bottles.

I heard from another friend this week. She said she had been out in her garden trying to remove some overgrown ivy and yucca plants. At every tug, she gritted her teeth and said, "Jo Ann!" I don't think it was a compliment. But at least she was doing something constructive.

PRUNING: A MISSION OF MERCY

I love to prune trees. Call it compulsive, call it power-hungry, call it whatever you want to call it.

I have three pairs of pruning shears: one in the garage, one in the kitchen, and one in the greenhouse. For larger branches, I use loppers. For high branches, we have a pruner on a long pole. It works by pulling a rope to close the blades. Higher than that, we hire someone to do, or leave the tree alone. It's not really safe to prune unless you can stand on the ground to do it. Professionals have the equipment, skill, and insurance to protect themselves and you.

This year, I bought a holster to put on a belt for my pruners. I actually strut around the place wearing it and snipping things. Now that's power.

About April, I get that urge. I don't know if it's the proper time, but it's when all the sprouts and suckers show on the trees. The time to prune is when it's needed, so that's what I do.

I can hear you saying, "What's a sucker?" That's what's growing in the crotch of another branch to the tree, or in the middle of a Y junction. Those will crowd the tree and overgrow it. Trees need air and sunlight to pass through, and less demand on their roots than allowing suckers would permit. Trust me.

Some people are afraid to prune, thinking they will ruin the tree. But once you realize that it actually improves the tree, it feels like a mission of mercy, like when you get a haircut!

Before and during pruning, take a second to cut the small branches up into small pieces and put them in a bucket for the compost pile.

So where to start? Let's imagine a small tree. First, never trim the leader. That's the main stem (trunk) of the tree. Unless you really want it to stop growing, which usually you don't. Second, never remove more than one-third of the branches at one time. That would shock the tree and could cause severe damage.

Cut off all the suckers (sprouts) around the base of the tree, and along the trunk up to the lowest branch. By the way, where is the lowest branch? It will never get higher than it is right now, so if you want to get your riding mower under it, and save your head from bruises, remove a few lower branches each year until it's high enough. Those branches will begin to droop as they get longer. It's a lot easier to remove them when they're small.

Now the easy part. Look at the branches. You will probably see a few that grow straight up from a main branch. These are called water sprouts. Cut them ALL off. Cut just outside the collar, which is a raised place next to the main branch.

Next, look for branches that cross each other. These will eventually rub together causing damage and disease. Pick the one you want to keep and remove the other one.

Look for any broken or damaged branches and remove them. You should already see a much-improved branch structure. Next come the more difficult decisions.

You will see some branches going from the tree at a right angle, the strongest joint. A branch that joins at a narrow angle (a Y, for example) will eventually split in a storm, or under the weight of snow and ice. Remove the branch with the narrow angle.

The rest is art. The goal is to open up the middle of the tree to let in air and light. Think about a robin being able to fly straight through the tree. It will look a little bare at first, but will soon fill in with leaves. Happy pruning!

GARDENING IS FOR THE BIRDS

As I write this, I'm watching a gentle spring rain fall outside. The grass is a beautiful green, trees are just beginning to open their buds, shrubs have hints of green at their base or their tips, my bluebird house has a customer, and the tulips and daffodils proudly announce another spring has arrived.

There are other signs, too. My dog Missy is rediscovering her digging habits. She likes to hollow out a sleeping place in the mulch next to the blueberries. From there, she can see the back door, the deer on the hill, and the neighbor's cat sneaking across the field to hunt mice. I don't have the heart to chase her out, so I don't plant anything in her spot.

A new sign of spring this year is my husband fussing about when to open the martin house. I got him a double decker last Christmas. It's installed with the openings plugged, as the book recommends.

We are not supposed to open it until early May when the sub-adults arrive in this area, but nearly every morning he says, "Do you think we should open it today?" We are both looking forward to their arrival.

My grandfather had a martin house that he built himself. Once when I was about 10 years old, he handed me a BB gun and asked me to shoot at the starlings around the martin house to scare them away. He went inside, probably thinking it would keep me busy for hours.

I remember taking aim, and BANG! One of the birds fell to the ground. I ran inside to tell Grandpa, "I shot one!" I shouted.

He looked surprised. "I'll bet you killed a martin," he said. I had. I was crushed. I felt terrible. I had harmed a gentle creature that my grandfather hoped to have live in his yard.

I can hear you thinking, "What's this have to do with gardening?" Birds are one of nature's ways of controlling the insect population and weed seeds — without chemicals. They eat thousands of harmful insects and weed seeds every day. Of course, they also eat a few worms and peck at my blueberries, but I don't mind. They even pecked at the plastic berries I put on my Christmas wreath last winter.

One summer we spent weeks watching a mockingbird sing and fly his little heart out up and down and in circles, trying to attract a mate. He woke us up every morning with his show. We used to pray some lady mockingbird would give him a tumble, and finally one did.

There's nothing better than waking up on a beautiful spring morning to a bird's cheery, "Thank you!"

COLD FRAMES SAVE YOU MONEY

The change in temperature this week has been a real blessing to us and to our gardens. It makes me think of fall, and that means it's time to make a cold frame. Here in Ohio, a cold frame is one way you can extend the growing season and start your own plants from seeds or cuttings.

A cold frame is a gizmo that sits on the ground with no bottom. The wooden or metal frame can be covered with clear flexible plastic sheeting, like a window frame without the glass. The frame is hinged to a sturdy wooden back that is partly buried into the soil. Sides are straight on the bottom, and sloped gradually down to meet the low front. All four sides are inserted into the ground for stability.

Actually, it's like a mini-greenhouse. Dig out the bottom so that you have room to add sand to it. Then add potting soil over the whole thing, or sand if you plan to plant into pots or containers. Put the seeds or seeded pots inside about April, and check often.

I first used mine to move seedlings from my kitchen table to the outdoors to harden them off. In the summer, my husband used the soft soil inside to grow perfectly straight carrots. Later, I tried cuttings inside to protect them from the drying winds. Once rooted, you can gradually move them to the house, then outside to a protected area, and finally to a permanent location. You also need a way to prop open the lid on hot sunny days so as not to burn the plants. Different sized rocks or wooden blocks do the trick. On a sunny day, temperatures inside can rise amazingly. You might want to keep a thermometer inside to keep a check on things. Raising the lid an inch or two does the trick. Just remember to close it in the evening.

How do I use it? Now I use it to put hardy shrubs in pots to protect them from wind and sunburn during their first winter. I use it to start seeds earlier than is possible outdoors. I use it to transfer plants I've started from cuttings to gradually get used to sun and shade. In other words, there are a lot of ways to use it. This fall, because our summer has not been wonderful, I hope to catch up on my veggie production by planting directly in the cold frame. Like the microwave in the kitchen, if you use it constantly, it's probably a good investment.

So what is a cold frame, you say? It's a low, enclosed planting bed that collects solar energy and protects delicate seedlings from damaging wind and cold. It's called a cold frame because it usually has no source of heat inside, though some well-rotted manure added to the soil will generate a considerable amount of heat for awhile. Also the sun, trapped by the clear top of sheet plastic or glass, adds heat to protect the plants. If it does have a source of heat, it's called a hot bed, not a cold frame.

It can protect plants from a hard freeze through November in this area, if it is managed and built correctly, and if the plants can withstand a light frost.

So in the fall, if you stick with plants like carrots, onions, lettuce, spinach, radishes, and other cold-tolerant plants, it's possible to have freshly-picked vegetables from it for Thanksgiving dinner - an easy way to impress your mother-in-law in time for her to adjust your Christmas present accordingly.

Cold frames can be made quite easily, and late summer is a good time to start. You can make them entirely from discarded materials, or you can buy a completed one from a gardening center or catalog. We made ours of concrete blocks laid end-to-end in a rectangle, and two layers deep. My husband built a cover with wood and clear corrugated fiberglass for it. He also built a wooden sloped arrangement to the top which holds the cover. The slope helps to catch sun and heat.

Many people use old window sashes or storm doors for this from the local salvage yard, but it is probably better to replace the glass with plastic for safety and weight reasons. Jim hinged ours and made a way to prop it open, but this isn't necessary.

We put a layer of potting soil and peat moss inside so that we could plant directly there, but you can just use flats and pots and set them on gravel or sand if you wish. I found that I usually use pots and flats anyway. We also put in several milk jugs of water as solar collectors during a cold or hot spell. The water in the jugs absorbs the solar heat, and releases it slowly later when the temperatures outside begin to drop. Likewise, when the temperature inside gets hot, they can absorb some of that heat as well, so they act as a neutralizer.

The cold frame can heat up on a sunny day, even when it's very cold outside. This will quickly kill tender seedlings, but is avoidable by opening the lid slightly to allow the heat to escape. If you're not home in the day, you may want to invest in an automatic hinge that opens at a specific temperature to prevent loss of plants, or just raise the lid every day during the time you'll be gone.

The most critical part of managing a cold frame is remembering to water inside. Because it's under a lid, the plants totally depend on you for water, and they dry out quickly. It's easy to forget in late October.

For a gardener, the best part of having a cold frame is allowing you to get your hands dirty growing things in March and November. That's enough for me.

START YOUR GARDENING NOW

April is the time in Ohio to get out into the fresh air and begin the new season. There are vegetables that can withstand some cold weather. So get into the garden early this year.

Spring veggies include cabbage, broccoli, spinach, peas and others. We are planting more greens like spinach and mesclun (a mixture of leafy greens) every week, as well as radishes and peas. I plan to try Swiss chard this year, and will check the book or the package for cold hardiness before I do.

Some flowers like cold weather too, and can be planted now. Pansies and sweet peas are examples. Don't bother covering them on a frosty night - they'll do fine unless it's a hard freeze.

It's too early to plant warm weather seeds or plants. If you're not sure, ask the nursery person. Once in Cleveland at a plant nursery, I asked an employee what the average frost-free date was up there. (It varies by location.) The young man, unfamiliar with the term, said there wasn't any "guaranteed" frost-free date. (Note: I didn't ASK for a guaranteed date.) He asked his boss and they BOTH looked at me strangely. I advised my friend to buy her plants elsewhere. All nursery staff should be aware of what the average frost-free date in their area is. The average frost-free date is the date at which half the time no frost occurred after that date in that area. This is a general guideline for all different areas, and in most of our county it is May 10. Remember, that still means that you may have to run out and cover your tomatoes for the night during a cold snap, but it's a good ball-park date to go by. There are maps of the USA showing these areas.

We have used cold protecting devices for starting our tomatoes, but found that they do better if we wait until the season really starts before we plant. Last year, we fussed over them for six weeks before discarding them and planting over at the normal planting time.

Spring is a good time for tasks you won't have time to do later. Getting gardening tools sharpened and oiled for the year is a smart move. This also a good time to divide perennials, and trim up any you didn't get done last fall.

I noticed a group of my daffodils all blooming on only one side of the house this spring. I'll wait until later in the season and divide them up. They've been there a long time, and the other spot has gotten shadier. It's time to move and divide them as well. Ditto for my hostas.

We spent an afternoon recently in our compost piles and found they were finished. We had several wheelbarrow loads of compost to gently spread around as an organic fertilizer. Areas benefitting were my new shrub bed, the vegetable and shade gardens, grapes, blueberries, raspberries, and strawberries. I sneaked two buckets out to put in the greenhouse for special projects.

I plan to take some starts from my myrtle bed and ivy cuttings to start on the hill. I pot them up in the greenhouse to develop roots, then gradually harden them off to outside weather.

In the greenhouse, I started seeds for tomatoes, privet, poppies, and alyssum. To have room, I moved some shrubs I wintered over in the greenhouse. In a couple weeks I can set them out to grow on another year, or to be permanently planted out. My daughter-in-law likes boxwood, so I have been nursing some for her for two years.

The best part of gardening now is the anticipation. Tulips are budding, trees are wearing a pale green mist, the grass has suddenly burst into color, and cherry trees are in bloom. How can you stay indoors when all this awaits?

THE ORGANIZED GARDENER

I am learning the benefits of record keeping in gardening. Two years ago, I bought a photo album, the kind with peel-back plastic that can hold full pages of photos and notes. I used it to hold designs of each year's garden, including early, mid-, and late stages. I also included plant care tags or catalogue descriptions of plants or seeds I purchased. Later, I added index cards with notes about production problems and result such as quantity produced, taste, etc. This was very helpful the following years as I made my plant and seed purchases.

But it didn't serve as a guide for me in the way of what I should be doing mid-April, for example, or what the weather was like at various periods of the year.

Last year for Mother's day, my husband got me a gardening journal. It has sections for ten years' entries on each calendar date. It also has areas to enter gardening purchases, tool lists, harvesting records, and other data.

I realize that not everyone is as compulsive as I am about records, and I confess that I gardened for many years without doing it. But a ten-year record of my efforts intrigues me. Had I kept this from the beginning, even in a notebook, I might've been a lot smarter. By now I'd be brilliant. Maybe.

What can you do right now? You can visit garden centers, dreaming of the beautiful setting you are creating. (Don't be disappointed if it doesn't measure up. It takes time to see the benefits.) You can clean out beds, move and divide things, and generally re-arrange. Try that perennial in another spot if it's not thriving where it is. Take a shovel or hatchet out, dig up that clump of Hosta or ornamental grass, and cut it into sections. Replant the sections, or give some away. These passalong plants, ones that are easily shared with gardening friends, can become a family tradition, much like heirloom tomatoes.

My Miscanthus grass, which is so beautiful during the winter above the goldfish pond with snow captured on its seed heads, was a gift from a neighbor who has now passed on. She regularly asked me how big around the clump was. It gets bigger every year, or rather it would if I didn't keep giving shovelfuls away. I do this to share her gift to me.

This year I plan to move the entire plant, and divide it into four sections to provide more design consistency. That sounds impressive, but it really means I want more of them throughout my garden.

There is only a short time left, approximately two weeks, until I can plant out things that are tender. I must finish these early tasks before then, so I have time to get all the plants in between mid-May and June 1.

Another thing I plan to do before the average frost-free date of May 10 is to shape some of my small shrubs and evergreens. I will shorten long shoots to make a nice shape and to encourage bushiness. I will trim my young evergreens to shape them. I did this last summer for the first time and was surprised to see how thick and green they became over the winter.

I know how busy you are - but a few minutes every day or so plus a bit of organizing can make a world of difference - trust me.

TAKE NOTES TO LOCAL NURSERY

If you haven't already, you will probably soon be standing amid a confusing array of plants at the local nursery, drenched in a fragrant smell and awash in colors and leaf texture. Temptations abound. If you're not careful, you'll come home with tons of things that struck your fancy, but don't match your landscape or your site. Ask me how I know this.

Before you go, take a walk around your lawn or the area you'll be planting, and bring a notebook. You may see bare spots that you'd like to fill. Write down where the spot is, and look at what's nearby. Is it surrounded by shrubs, or sitting next to a hot driveway? Does it get sun all day, or less than a few hours? Is it on a slope and dries out quickly? What plants are next to it that you'd like to match or contrast with? Check out the colors nearby, and decide what you'd like. Don't forget that plants change throughout the year, so an area that's blue in the spring might be orange in the fall. Not likely, but a good example. Also consider when you would like something blooming there. For example, if the bed has a mass of daffodils, but after that is pretty boring, you might want a later perennial or a shrub that blooms in the summer and offers fall color as well.

Finally, think about texture and foliage color. Do you have a lot of light, feathery foliage, and think the site would benefit from a large-leafed bold plant? Or perhaps you have many dark greens most of the year, or some shade part of the day and would like to lighten it up with some variegated foliage. Don't forget the many shades of green that are available, and the many leaf shapes. The foliage is what is present most of the year, so it's often more important than the flowers.

After you work up this spot, move on to the next. When you have a complete list, add other things you might need, such as mulch, soil amendments, tools, and seeds. Many plants will grow easily from seed, and actually do better that way. They're a lot easier on the pocketbook, too.

You might want to get a large pot or two, and some potting soil. Those seeds can end up as a beautiful complement or accent for your patio or entryway in a large container. A pot can stay in your living room or kitchen till mid-May, and do fairly well if you can get it some sun. Then it can go outdoors when the danger of frost is past. You can move it in case of frost.

Last thing - ask the rest of the family what they would like to plant this year.

REVENGE OF THE PRUNING WOMAN

I did it. I had my first pruning spasm of the year. Sadly, it happened during a spring rain, so I lost my hairdo in the process, but it was a good feeling. For some reason, every year about this time, I feel a sort of primal urge to snip and thin young trees to encourage strong growth and eliminate clutter. So I strap on my belt and holster, slide in my favorite pruners, and - TA DAH! - Pruning Woman!

Pruning Woman knows no fear - she leaps over small bushes to reach those sapling trees. She addresses the task by slowly circling the tree, perusing every branch to the tip.

My first task, should I choose to accept it, and I always do, is to remove the lowest circle of branches. This is "limbing up" the tree. I always do this on young trees for several years, so that eventually the branches reach a good height. For a shade tree, for example, I would cut two to four branches off the bottom every year until the lowest branch is well above my head. That way, when the branches are 8 to 10 inches thick, I don't crack my head trying to mow under them. Also, the house isn't hidden behind a jungle of branches.

The next step is to trim any suckers (sprouts) coming up from the base of the tree, and any small sprouts on the trunk up to the first branches. At this point, I step back to admire the clean trunk.

I now use my intellectual capacity (such as it is) to thin out that tree for strength, beauty, and production. I cut off all water sprouts on all the branches I can reach. Those are the ones that grow straight up from the side, or lateral, branches. Left undone, they will eventually cross any horizontal or sloping branch. Not a pretty or healthy sight. I also trim off any broken branches, and remove any that rub against or cross another branch.

By this time, I have a wagonload of trimmings and a tree that has clean lines and an open look - one that a robin can fly straight through. I love this part. Of course, if you're a real tree lover - and who isn't? - you're probably thinking the tree is scalped. But the leaves will fill back in, and the tree will be much healthier for the work. Trust me.

About a month ago, my sister-in-law Beth told me she had two pear trees, and one bore sweet juicy fruit, while the other bore sour fruit.

"Have you pruned it?" I asked. (I've seen those trees.)

"No, I haven't pruned them," she said, a little defensively.

It probably has nothing to do with it, but maybe she will this year.

Being Pruning Woman is an awesome responsibility.

MOWING, TREES, AND HOPE

I love to mow - there are so many benefits. It takes a lot of time, but it gets me in touch with every part of the lawn. I see things up close that are easy to overlook during the normal hurly-burly of my day. This week, for example, I startled a crow, who let me know he was not pleased. I saw several damaged pines. Mentally, I calculated to the hum of the lawn mower what might be the trouble. One could have been damaged by deer. They like to rub their itchy antlers on the trees in the spring, and often rub the bark right off, using most of the branches on one side of the tree. Not a pretty sight.

I also saw Scotch pines with branches displaying a bottle-brush effect, old needles nearly gone, and only the new ones at the tip looking healthy. I remembered those striped caterpillars there earlier in the spring, and also noticed as I mowed past the scotch pines that insects flew up and scattered. After a little research, I learned it was probably European Pine Sawfly, thanks to the County Extension Service. Their material says the trees won't die, but they won't be beautiful either. Will they recover eventually? The fact-sheet doesn't address this. I will watch them closely for further damage, and if they don't recover their appearance, out they go.

Our hillside, once covered with dogwoods, is losing more this year, I see. First one branch fails to develop leaves, then another, until finally the entire tree is lost. We have been losing two or three mature dogwoods each year. I now know the cause is anthracnose, a disease for which there is no cure. I will miss these beauties in the spring with their cream-colored blossoms, so unpretentious and sturdy-looking. But they are even more beautiful in the fall when the entire tree turns a burgundy red. That's when I really love mowing on our hill. I often stop the mower just to enjoy the view.

While these were worrisome developments, I was given a gift at the same time. All over the hillside, tiny oak trees spread their first leaves just over the grass. Our squirrel friend who monopolizes the bird feeder must have had a burst of energy last fall. His planting style was very similar to my husband's: three feet apart and sometimes in a straight line. Probably 50 baby trees were growing on the hillside, most of which I mowed off, both by intent or accident. I saved 20 or so, knowing someday maybe our hillside will have a new look.

Last year while mowing, I saw a huge bird flying very high. I strained to see what it was. Just in front of the wings, the body seem to stop - a headless bird flying powerfully at great heights? Surely it couldn't be a bald eagle. That's ridiculous. I must be seeing things. Later, I learned that not only do we have bald eagles in Ohio, we have them in Licking County, courtesy of Buckeye Lake. This was undoubtedly one of those. I hope to see one again one day. He/she was flying from the Licking River toward Buckeye Lake.

(UPDATE: Probably 20 years later, we stopped at our brother-in-law's house one day and when we rounded the corner of his house, he was walking toward us with probably 8 to 10 bald eagles flying around him only a few feet in the air. I said, "Wow!" It was the only word that came to mind. It was a magnificent sight. The eagles, not my brother-in-law.

He replied, "Oh they're around here all the time." A side note - he lives very close to the Licking River. A second note - I suspect he feeds them or they wouldn't have been surrounding him like that. Nevertheless, I was a sight I will never forget.

Back to mowing. I frequently find new mounds or holes, probably caused by creatures I don't want to know about. I have mowed over yellow jacket nests, and blithely passed by several times, wondering what was buzzing about. Luckily, my husband offered to mow about that time, and quit after his first pass.

A pair of white boxes entertains me this year as I mow. My husband has become a beekeeper. I'm thankful each time out that these are not the African style bees - "killer bees" as the media people call them. Our bees peacefully go about their business as I pass by, unlike the African bees who resent tractor noises. This week I saw a group of bees collected at the entrance to the hive. They were not passing in and out as usual, and I motioned to my husband to take a look. "They're cleaning it," he said. I watched for a little while, thinking it looks like someone running a vacuum cleaner back and forth across a carpet. It occurred to me that I probably should be cleaning mine.

But I much prefer mowing.

WATCHING FOR BLOOMS IS A GUESSING GAME

Gardening in the spring is all about anticipation. The sky bulges with moisture, biding its time before it baptizes seeds and plants with life-giving water. Carnations reach upward, tight buds held high above feathery foliage, their color kept a secret until the next sunny day when both fragrance and color will be obvious.

My hillside garden sports a few small plants whose fate is yet unknown: pregnant with swelling zucchini or eaten by deer and rabbits in the evening damp. Who knows?

One lone stem of Oak Leaf Hydrangea peeks out of the pachysandra by the door. Planted last year and forgotten, it hid beneath the ground cover as it gathered strength. According to the old saying, the first year it sleeps, the second year it creeps, and the third year it leaps. Perhaps next year it will develop a strong presence and even sport lacy white panicle flowers shaped like an ice cream cone. I will enjoy the first flower, and remind myself that this shrub started with a snip of my pruning shears and months of attention to its needs.

Dahlias, Calla Lilies, and Veronicas lie hidden beneath inches of soil and mulch in the flowerbed. Planted too late, I only hope they reach their peak this year. Vines curl at the bottom of the post or tree where they have been planted, and can't seem to find their strength for the summer. Later, after they have struggled awhile, I will help them.

Just this week, Jim and I watched as our squirrel friend sat on the head of the concrete goose. His tail draped down the neck, much like a fashion model's fur-trimmed hat. Kodak helped us preserve the moment. Soon he turned toward us, apparently satisfied that no one approached his perch from the yard. He came directly under our window and began to dig in the mums beneath us. He occasionally pulled up a root or leaf and tasted it. Not what he was looking for, he discarded these and kept digging. Soon he found what he wanted: a walnut. This went into his mouth and he headed back to his nesting tree.

Jim said, "I wonder how he remembers where all his nuts are hidden."

I didn't know. But I thought it might be the same way I know where all my plants are. I just keep thinking about them.

GARDEN SCORE: JIM 0, ME 0

Since I have received a number of inquiries (one) as to how "Jim's garden" is doing, I decided to bring you up to date. Even with all his objections, and even with temperatures dropping to 14 degrees the night after planting, most are up. The spinach, romaine, and radishes have all sprouted, and glitter in the morning sun. The onions, peas, and carrots are taking their time deciding if it really is spring yet, but I am sure they will eventually take the plunge and appear above ground. Even if we have a frost, and we probably will, these vegetables can take it. In fact, they prefer cooler temperatures. By June or so, they will be done, and we can plant a different second crop for the fall. I won this one.

My greenhouse didn't fare as well. The morning after planting, I went up to check on things and do some more planting. In the propagation bed were shells of squash and cucumber seeds scattered around the pots, and large gaping holes in the potting soil. I hurried over to the other bench and drew back the plastic. This one was worse. Soil had been thrown out of the pots onto the heating mats, and damage was everywhere. We had a mouse in the greenhouse.

We were at war. I enlisted Jim, and he moved into the procurement phase. It was the age-old dilemma: Should we use chemicals and prevent the crop damage, or forego the chemicals and suffer the damage to the crops? I knew that a mouse at this stage could render the greenhouse useless for us. We opted for the poison. He promised to get some that day.

Any mouse that locates a greenhouse as a home can live like a king. Warmth, water, green leaves all winter, and wonderful nooks and crannies for nesting places make it a veritable mouse heaven. Jim, true to his word, brought home the poison and carefully placed it out of the way where moisture probably wouldn't find it. Next morning he went up to check. He saw a mouse escaping along the bench, but couldn't get to it in time. The battle turned to open warfare at this point, but the mouse only lost a bit of its tail. When I checked the pots later, I saw green granular items. These, Jim confirmed, were bits of rat poisons that the mouse had hidden. I was uneasy about having poison in my planting pots, wondering what else it would affect. Jim promised to try a less dangerous method.

Day three of the battle began with me. Checking the water level of the pots, I saw that Jim had laid a piece of scrap paper on top of a clear plastic tub that I had scavenged for planting some seeds. It was blocking the light, which wouldn't hurt anything at this stage, but would as soon as the seeds germinated, so I picked it up. I knew immediately that it was a mistake, as all four fingers on top of the card were firmly stuck to the surface. Without thinking, I impatiently grabbed it with my other hand. Now both hands were stuck. This was obviously Jim's non-lethal method of fighting mice. He had caught a huge one this time. Suddenly a picture flashed in my mind: Red Skelton fighting off a sticky sheet, and getting more entangled with each move. Eventually I used my mind instead of my instinct, and got myself extricated from the sticky mousetrap.

No further evidence of a mouse has been found, but I have no way to tell which pots still have seeds and which don't. My hunch is that we no longer have squash or cucumbers planted, but this is easily remedied.

The other spring task we completed last week was to fertilize our lawn with a product that includes crabgrass preventer. You still have time to do this, though not a lot. Crabgrass preventer must be used before it germinates, and warm weather marks the end of its effectiveness. Our product said to use March through May, but I believe that earlier is better, in life and in crabgrass. We are sorely out of practice using a drop spreader, so I have fears that our lawn will be striped from overlaps and gaps left during the application.

I guess we could claim it's a new game called lawn tic-tac-toe.

SPRING COMETH - PLANT THE SEEDS OF PROGRESS

Much satisfaction can be gained by getting a head start on your planting. I finally started my season in earnest this weekend. I bought seeds for cold crops and spring flowers. I managed to convince Jim to plant the seeds in the vegetable garden while I held forth in the greenhouse. Jim grumbled that it was too early, the leaves weren't totally decomposed in the garden, the seeds would rot, the NCAA tournament was coming on, etc. Even so, he planted onion sets, spinach, carrots, romaine lettuce and peas. Missy, our black lab, stretched out on the warm bricks of the patio and watched him work. I hope he wasn't right about the seeds rotting. Snow flew immediately after he finished, and the next morning, our thermometer read 14 degrees.

Even so, two neat rows of rich brown soil catch my eye as I look out the kitchen window. When the seeds sprout and the soil warms, we will again scoot the mulch up to the plants.

While he worked, I entered the greenhouse where it really was spring inside. Plants largely ignored all winter sprouted tall healthy green shoots, and I let them have a drink of water in appreciation. Others had given up the ghost, and were banished to the compost pile to make room for a new generation.

Next, I dug out my seedling pots from last year, and scrubbed them in a tub of bleach water to kill any yucky bacteria. The potting soil had dried out during the winter, so I put a couple of inches of water in the plastic dishpan I keep for that purpose, and set some six packs of potting soil in it to soak. Once peat moss is dry, it is very difficult to re-wet. As this process began, I donned my planting apron. This, I have learned, saves a lot of muddy fingerprints on my clothes. In the pockets of the apron are some plot stakes, a marker, some pruning shears, and my gardener's knife, assuming I returned them all the last time I used them.

The next step was to pull out all the seeds, both those newly purchased, and those leftover from last year. I had collected some redbud seeds from our tree last fall, and Jim found a nut that a squirrel forgot to bury. The nut spent all winter in our refrigerator, and soon will find a new home in a small pot in the greenhouse. I sorted the seed packets. Many were left over from last year, and I discarded most of these, along with all the pots that were cracked or broken. I made a mental note to discard some more things every time I come up to check on the plants, which will be often during the next six weeks.

Next, I selected the packets to plant. Some had a small envelope inside which doubled as a seeder, making it easy to gently shake the seeds into each planting square. If the seeds were very tiny, I placed many in each square. Later, I will thin or transplant these to other pots as they get their second set of leaves. The large seeds, like moonflower and morning glory, I placed two to a square. I generally cover the seeds about two times deeper than the size of the seeds. As I worked, I added more six packs and soil to the water pan to wet, and carefully marked each six pack with a plant stake, the variety and date planted. I moved the seeded and marked trays to the heat mats on the benches, gently sprayed the soil again for insurance, and pulled the plastic cover over the bench, to hold the moisture in the air. This helps to reduce my heating costs, because I can keep the greenhouse cooler.

Gradually, many dark squares covered the mat and the propagation bench. I set the heat mat at 65 degrees and pulled the greenhouse door tightly closed behind me.

There's only one thing more satisfying than a row of newly canned vegetables on my shelf - and that's the spring seeds planted.

WHERE'S GLOBAL WARMING
WHEN WE NEED IT?

Any gardener knows the influence of climate on growing things. It's difficult not to notice when you're on your knees in wet mud, your nose six inches from the soil. Reading the seed packet you got from the garden center, you see "Plant as soon as the soil has warmed." But when is that? Of course, I could buy one of those soil thermometers, but I was always afraid the neighbors would see me.

The answer, of course, is that it varies. Some are warm springs, some cold. The good news is that things happen in the same order, and students of nature have been able to notice this order simply by paying attention. Planting potatoes on Good Friday, or peas on St. Patrick's Day may not always work, but if you pay attention to the signs as you plant, you may be able to figure out a time that's best. Did you plant peas when your daffodils were in bloom and have a wonderful crop? Or were the oak trees leafed out the size of a cat's ear? Was your favorite shrub in bloom? Write these things down in your garden journal, and then note the quantity and quality of production that year. You are keeping one, right? Once you document that a certain sign is a good time to plant pears, for example, you can safely rely on that sign to hold, regardless of the date on the calendar. If you then move to Tennessee, you can still rely on that sign to plant, as the sequence is the same, regardless of the date on the calendar.

So how do you begin to pay attention to nature around you? You might want to record the date you planted first in your vegetable garden this year, and what was happening around you as you did. Figure out the projected germination and production times from the seed packet. Then record the first date you actually harvest the first produce. Also record the date you first see the robins, the blooming times of forsythia, daffodils, and pussy willows, the last snow, and so on. See if any of those times coincide with other things. You'll get smarter every year, and will begin to understand nature's clock. While the weather doesn't always match the calendar, it is always consistent with nature. Use nature as your guide, not the calendar.

The climate changes affect us as well as the plants. While I'm not an expert on plant behavior, I have begun to notice the weather's effect on people. As a young teacher, I noticed that students on some days were squirellier than others. (My apologies to the squirrels.) Then I noticed that so were the teachers. It seemed to happen on days it was about to rain or storm. Drivers, too, were affected, as driving was more aggressive on those days. I wondered if there were more murders or crimes of assault on those days. Could it be the dropping barometric pressure, I wondered? Hmmmm. Would someone research those ideas please?

Another observation came as I drove to work on a beautiful sunny spring day, a high barometric pressure day. I missed my turn the way to work. Twice. What was going on? Was it just the beautiful day taking my attention, or was it something else? Drivers were far more polite that day, as were students and teachers. Maybe there was something to this.

Why do I mention this? We are all biological creatures. If the sun and moon and weather affect our plants, they certainly affect us, too. As you study nature this spring, pay attention to your own responses as well. It might make you a better gardener. Then you can bore your grandchildren with it.

PLANTS LUSH WITH SENTIMENT

One of the benefits of doing a column on gardening is that some very interesting questions come up that tell me what real gardeners are worrying about. One question in particular reminded me of how plants become emotionally intertwined with our lives.

A lady called and asked if I had ever heard of a night blooming cereus. As luck would have it, I had. My mother-in-law, who loved plants, had one for many years. She often talked about it and showed it to us when we were over. The cereus is a succulent (cactus for you horticulturally challenged) that blooms at night. Hers was in a large pot and was about four to five feet tall, as I remember. She would carefully lug it outdoors in the summer and back indoors in the fall, until one time she left it outside a little too late in the season, and an early frost ended its tenure in her life. I remembered that she was very proud of it, especially when it sported its pale yellow blooms.

The caller brought back all these memories, as I told her that, yes, I was familiar with it. She said her plant was huge, but that it hadn't bloomed for a couple of years and wondered if I had any suggestions. She was very attached to the plant, and she was trying to take very good care of it. I questioned her about its location, and how much sun it received. She said it faced the south and west side or her house, and that there were no trees or other light blockers that direction. She also moved it outside when weather permitted. I assumed it was getting enough light.

I asked about watering habits. Succulents store liquid in their leaves - that's why they are so thick and leathery - and they don't like excessive water. Good practice for these plants dictates that the soil dry out totally before watering again. Then they can be watered thoroughly, but should never stand in water, or they will turn to mush in short order. She passed in this area too.

Her father, who apparently hated the plant, had severely cut it back after his wife died. It had sent branches far and wide, and he wanted it contained. This, though, had been a couple of years earlier, and I didn't think it would still affect the blooming. Some plants set blooms on old growth, and these will decline to bloom for a year or more after a cutback, until the new growth turns into old, as we all do eventually. I thought enough time had passed to cover this contingency. On the other hand, sometimes if a plant is badly overgrown, a severe pruning can rejuvenate it, if done properly. I hoped this was the case, and that recovery would occur shortly after our discussion. That would make me look really good.

I asked about fertilizing. She hadn't done this, and the plant had been potted for a long time. I recommended she try to find a fertilizer for blooming cacti. Also, repotting the plant could improve it.

I'm afraid I wasn't much help, but I hoped she enjoyed the reminiscing about the cereus. I know I did.

GET A HEAD START ON PLANTING

Spring - ah, the season of propagation. You're probably dreaming of planting healthy green plants in dark, fluffy soil. Perhaps you're seeing yourself poking seeds in small pots, growing your own annuals and vegetables from scratch this year.

If you are, April 1st is a good date to start. This is six weeks before the frost-free date in this area, or May 15. The frost-free date is the average date of the last frost. Note that this means that frost half of the time occurs even after that date, so be ready to protect things. Six weeks' growing time is a general rule for plant development before planting outside, but you should check each seed packet for exact times.

If you would like to start your own seeds, you might want to build or invest in a small propagation house. The purchased ones usually offer bottom heat and a clear plastic vented top, like a miniature greenhouse. You can make your own with a low wooden or metal box, a polyethylene cover with supports, vented on the ends. You can purchase small bench mats for bottom heat. Why bottom heat? Many seeds need soil warmth to germinate. Bottom heat and cool air above usually imitates our spring outdoor conditions as the dark soil warms in the sun. The plastic cover retains some of the humidity to keep the plants turgid (stiff) in their tender stage, and the venting is crucial to prevent excessive heat buildup. (Think of your car on a sunny day.)

Once the plants have developed the second set of leaves, you can start venting more, and gradually acclimate these to outdoor temperatures. On a windy day, though, provide some protection so plants don't dry out or break. You will probably need to bring the plants in at night for warmth.

A word of advice - use several seeds in each pot, and remove the weakest ones as they grow. This takes courage and determination, but if you don't, you'll have 3 or 4 weak plants instead of one strong one. Also, many seeds may come in one package. You don't have to plant them all just because they're there. Potting soil, pots, and especially bench space are expensive. You probably don't really need 1000 Marigolds or 250 tomatoes. I know - you're thinking, "I can give them away!" This is a charitable thought, but would take care of a few plants. It would be far easier - and less expensive - to not plant them at all.

When you're planting seeds, try soaking a couple of Buckeyes, acorns, maple seeds, and redbud seeds for 24 hours, and planting them, too. Imagine a 40' oak tree started with your own hands. Talk about delusions of grandeur!

EARLY SPRING WORKOUT

Between bouts of snow and bone-chilling winds, it's obvious that spring is not far away. Though the robins aren't yet back, the sky is brightening, light lasts longer each day, daffodils are peeking up through the leaves, and animals are getting smashed on country roads. Ah, wonderful spring.

One thing that you can do right now is to think about re-seeding any bare spots in your lawn. The natural freezing and thawing that occurs often in unpredictable spring weather is a great way for seeds to sink into the soil to be ready to sprout at the first sign of warm weather. Just buy some good seed and sprinkle it over the spots that are thin. That's it! No watering, raking, mulching, fertilizing, etc. Mother Nature will do the rest.

Another early spring project is to get those pruning shears and saws out to prune your trees. Take that first beautiful spring day when you can't stand to be indoors any longer and go walk around your trees. (Hint: If you can't reach the branches, it's best to hire someone to do this for you.) The first thing to remember is never to remove more than one-third of the branches at any one time. If a tree has not been pruned for a very long time, it might take you three years to completely revitalize it. Translation: Hire a tree trimmer.

First, look for the "water sprouts" - any branches that are growing straight up. These will obviously cross over other branches as they grow and cause problems later, and will probably not bear any fruit or flowers regardless. Cut all those off, leaving the little collar, or raised area next to the main branch. Next, remove any damaged or broken collars. Studies have shown that the collar provides a natural healing process, which is far better than the wound paint we used to use. So never cut a branch off flush to the tree. Also, never leave a stub sticking out that will attract pests and insects, and thus damage the tree. These also can injure someone, as I learned years ago. I had only brought my loppers out, and couldn't cut the branch near the collar with them, as the branch was too large. I opted to cut it off further out where it was smaller around, and had to leave a foot-long stub, intending to finish the job later with a saw. My husband, hurrying to answer the phone, ran his head into it, and a trip to the emergency room was in order for stitches. He reminds me of this every spring.

If you have branches very low to the ground, you might want to "limb them up", as we call it, or cut them off to the height you want. These will never move any higher than they are now, and if you need to walk or mow under them, this is definitely in order. Remove one or two per year until the bottom limb reaches the desired height.

Next, step back to study the tree's structure for crossing branches or those that will cross if allowed to grow for a few years. It's a lot easier to cut these when they're a half-inch thick than when they're eight inches thick. If you think you have removed a third of the tree's branches at this point, stop until the fall or next spring. If not, continue by general thinning of the tree's center. Look for the strongest joint, which is the one most nearly perpendicular to the tree. A branch with a V joint is much weaker and more likely to split when loaded with ice or snow, or when a windstorm comes up. Aim for level branches, and an open center so that sun and air can get in. This tree will be happier, healthier, and more productive that those overcrowded, choked ones who haven't tasted a pruner or saw since they first put root to soil. The tree will look a little thin until it fills with leaves, but then you should see an improvement in its general health. Roger Swain of "Victory Garden" says to open it up so a robin could fly straight through it. I like that description best.

Finishing this task now during the cold weather and before the sap comes up will produce less stress for the tree, and it will quickly recover after it breaks its dormancy. It should improve your heart rate, too.

Another early spring task is to trim the ornamental grasses and any dormant plants that the winter didn't convince to lay over. A general clean-up of the flowerbeds will make them and you feel better. It's been a long winter - a little exercise is good for the soul, the body and the garden.

TIME IS NEAR FOR HEAD START ON PLANTING

Spring - ah, the season of propagation. You're probably dreaming of planting healthy green plants in fluffy soil. Perhaps you're seeing yourself poking seeds in small pots, growing your own annuals and vegetables from scratch this year.

If you are, April 1st is a good date to start. This is six weeks before the frost-free date in this area, May 15. The frost-free date is the average date of the last frost in the area. Note that this means that frost occurs half the time even after that date, so be ready to protect things. Six weeks growing time is a general rule for plant development before planting outside, but you should check each seed packet for exact times.

If you would like to start your own seeds, you might want to build or invest in a small propagation house. The purchased ones usually offer bottom heat and a clear plastic vented top, like a miniature greenhouse. You can make your own with a low wooden or metal box, a polyethylene cover with supports, vented on both ends. You can purchase small bench mats for bottom heat. Why bottom heat? Many seeds need soil warmth to germinate. Bottom heat and cool air above usually mimics our spring outdoor conditions as the dark soil warms in the sun. The plastic cover retains some of the humidity to keep the plants turgid in their tender stage, and the venting is crucial to prevent excessive heat buildup. (Think of your car on a sunny day.)

Once the plants have developed the second set of leaves, you can start venting more and gradually acclimate these to outdoor temperatures. On a windy day, though, provide some protection so plants don't dry out or break. You will probably need to bring the plants in at night for warmth.

A word of advice - use several seeds in each pot, and remove the weakest ones. This takes courage and determination, but if you don't, you'll have 3 or 4 weak plants instead of one strong one. Also, many seeds may come in one package. You don't have to plant them all just because they're there. Potting soil, pots and especially bench space are expensive. You probably don't really need 1,000 marigolds or 250 tomatoes. I know - you're thinking, "I can give them away!" Charitable, but you'll probably give away 10. It's far easier and cheaper to not plant them at all.

When you're planting seeds, try soaking a couple of buckeyes, acorns, maple seeds, and redbud seeds for 24 hours and planting them too. Imagine a 40' Oak tree started with your own hands. Talk about delusions of grandeur!

GARDENER HAS MUMS ON HER MIND

Karla writes: *Do you have any advice on propagation of mums? I take cuttings of mums in late May or early June to produce fall mums, with some success. This past fall, I brought* *some potted mums into my greenhouse because I read you should take cuttings of mums in February to get bigger plants for fall. I must be doing something wrong because these mums are all dried and dead, even though I water them. The spring before, (much warmer weather), I was surprised with growth in pots I had stored in the barn over the winter. Should I have left them out in a colder place? The greenhouse temperature ranges from 54 to 65 degrees during the day.*

I also would like to have connection with other hobby greenhouse owners so that I could learn without so much trial and error. My greenhouse is 8 x 10 and glass. One thing I have learned is that I must start my seeds 3-4 weeks earlier than the package says to have bloom when the commercials greenhouses are selling blooming plants.

Karla: What great questions!

I have propagated mums by cuttings - probably in June. They are not as delicate as in May, and not hardened off too much as in August. All this depends on the cultivar. Check at the library for details on yours. I'm not concerned about blooms by fall - I'm willing to wait another year for them to gain size.

If you bought those mums in pots, you need to know that some florist mums are not in the natural cycle. That is, they have been forced to bloom early, and will not likely survive the winter. I don't know about cuttings from them, but I wouldn't waste my time, bench space, or potting soil. I always use mums from my flowerbeds for cuttings. At least that way I know they're hardy for this area, and that I like the color.

It's hard to say about the mums you brought inside. The greenhouse may be overheated. I keep mine at a cool

45 degrees during the winter, and I use passive solar to even out temp swings (large, dark trash cans full of water, and flagstones absorb heat during the day and release it during the night). Many plants actually need a dormant period for survival. Outside they would get that, even in a warmer winter. A cool greenhouse is fine for most plants other than tropical ones, and is much cheaper to run. Geraniums, cyclamen and mums all flourish in cool temperatures. I've had geraniums blooming in winter at these temperatures. An easy way to create a small heated place is to use heated mats on your bench, and then cover the bench loosely with clear plastic. Presto! Small greenhouse.

Finally, please DON'T try to have bloom when the nurseries do. They do that because people like to buy blooming plants. Plants need time to develop strong leaves and stems before they bloom. I usually pinch the blooms from annuals when I plant them. It saves some of the energy from blooming to developing the rest of the plant, like roots. If you are growing plants to sell, that's different.

Your most intriguing comment was wishing you had contact with other hobby greenhouse owners. That's a great idea. Readers, are you interested? If so, email me or write me care of The Advocate.

OLD PLANTS AND BUSY GARDENERS

I am really excited this week. I am expecting a landscaper to come and re-do my front flower bed. We liked the design, and decided to do half of it this year. Hopefully, the second part can be finished in the spring.

In preparation, we have moved a few plants, cleaned out two small areas, and done a lot of talking, but little action. Time doesn't allow us to do the stuff we used to enjoy. Someday again, we will be doing the exercise part, but for now, someone else is. As a respecter of skilled tradesmen, we recognize the talent and experience that a landscaper has, and are willing to pay him or her for that. It's worth it to have an attractive landscape that will only improve with age.

No landscape, however, can last forever. Plants get old, damaged, and overgrown and we have to face that fact and pull them out. Bigger is not always better. Crowded is not attractive. Windows should be clear of plants to let the light and view in, and so that bad guys have no place to hide. Often, as I drive down country roads or icy streets, I notice evergreens in front or at the sidewalk that started out as small shrubs, and have grown to miniature trees where no trees were intended. The trunks bare and twisted, the tops a ball of green much like a poodle after a bad pompadour haircut - I'm embarrassed for them. Just cut them down, dig them out, and give them a decent burial. Everyone will thank you for it.

And those shrubs marked "dwarf"? Yes, they'll grow slowly, but they'll not stop growing at 18 or 24 inches. Plants grow. That's what they DO. If they don't, they die. Just like people. So don't expect a plant to last 50 years unless it's an Oak tree. Those are champions made for the long haul.

Everything else has to go eventually, sooner rather than later. Nothing gives me more satisfaction than trimming or cutting back and, yes, even eliminating a plant that's past its prime. Sound heartless, doesn't it?

I used to try to grow Boston ferns in my home and had great difficulty. They dropped their leaves and looked as if they just survived a street fight. But then a lady who had the most beautiful fern I ever saw in her home told me the secret of raising them.

"My Grandma had a Dixie cup near hers, and put one Dixie cup of water on it every day. It always looked like this."

Never too little. Never too much. Brilliant.

Soon my fern went crazy. I drank ice water every night, and put the ice on the plant. Like people, when it got the love and attention it needed, it responded with grace.

I put it in bigger and bigger pots until it took one whole corner of my living room. Years later, it started to lose leaves again no matter what care I took. It sent out mounds of tendrils looking for new soil. It tried too hard. Finally, it went to the compost pile. I miss it, but the living room looks better.

TREE ABUSE ABOUNDS IN OUR COUNTY

(Support group starting soon)

This month I have seen severe cases of tree abuse. Those of you who are guilty know who you are, and will get an invitation to the support group soon. Not only are the trees severely at risk, but the appearance makes me embarrassed for them.

One example was huge pile of cypress mulch around a 12" diameter tree. Cypress mulch is from redwood trees, and will not rot down for years. The mulch was about 16 inches deep, yes 16 inches, and about four feet in diameter. The huge pile was in the front yard of a home near a city street. I imagine the mice, chipmunks or ground squirrels as my husband calls them, and even the rabbits love this "diner" for tree bark. They love to burrow under the mulch and head right for the tree. Enough of this will kill the tree eventually. While I mulch my trees, I keep the height at 2 to 3 inches deep, and pull it back from the trunk itself.

Another case was a beautiful shade tree in a front yard. What caught my eye while I waited for a red light was the attractive bed of Hostas, ferns, and other shade plants beneath the tree. Next, I noticed 6" tall row of flat stones, in a large circle surrounding the tree and enclosing the plants. Before the light turned red, I imagined a homeowner bemoaning the roots sticking out of the ground, and hitting on the idea of dumping topsoil on it and making a large bed for shade plants. The bed was beautiful but the loss of the tree will be tragic. If roots are near the surface, it's because they want to be, and they don't want an extra 12 inches of topsoil there. A homeowner can kill a tree with kindness. Don't be tempted.

An interstate where I travel occasionally has a row of very attractive flowering trees. At the base of each one is an ugly black 4" drain pipe sticking out of the ground a few inches. My eye is invariably drawn to the pipes rather than the trees. I have pondered this for a couple of years now. I think that someone decided one of two things: Either that it would be a good way to ensure the trees either could be easily watered, or that we decide to be generous by replacing the clay soil with a much "nicer" topsoil or peat mixture. Again, don't be tempted.

Most horticulturists now recommend simply crumbling up the soil that comes out of the hole, and putting it back in around the tree without additions or amendments. The drain pipe is a misguided attempt to help the tree. What would be better would be to plant strong native trees in the natural way and let nature take its course. If trees needed a drain pipe, they would all have one.

I have a slide of two gorgeous trees that have been "topped", a horrible practice that used to be in fashion where all of the branches are cut stud-like to reduce the height. I'm not sure what the logic is, but I know that it is not only harmful to the health of the tree - it also makes them look ridiculous, sort of like my son the time I decided to save a few bucks by giving him a haircut. My mother-in-law rubbed his head and said it looked like an old mule's head. I threw away the clippers after that. Tree companies that are willing to do this ought to be - well, you know.

Please don't abuse your trees. They are 50 or more years of time invested in your property, and they are good citizens. They provide cooling shade in summer, allow warm sun through in winter, and provide oxygen and clean air for all of us through their leaves. The loss of a tree is a very sad thing which takes many, many years to correct, and affects an entire neighborhood.

SUCCESS UNDER THE MIST

Two evenings ago, I ran up to the greenhouse to check on the last few cuttings that hadn't yet rooted.

I had checked them daily for four weeks, and still no sign of roots at the bottom or sides of the potting soil. During the hot spell, though, I had been negligent and not been to the greenhouse for two or three days.

Most of the cuttings done the same day had long ago rooted, but the beauty berry (callicarpa) and the trumpet vines were stubborn. I had an inkling they were rooting even though I couldn't see any, because the tops were green and healthy. You say, of course they're rooting in that case. Not necessarily. I have had plants produce new leaves on top and still no roots.

There is no harm to the plants if you gently place two fingers on either side of the stem, flat against the potting soil, and softly tap on the bottom side of the pot to dislodge the clump from the pot. Then it's easy to inspect the sides and bottom of the clump for roots. These showed healthy roots.

After about an hour's initial work with cuttings, hormones, and four weeks' care under the mist, I now have about four dozen baby shrubs in pots outside the greenhouse. In a few months, they will be ready to plant.

REFLECTIONS FROM A GARDENER

There are some things I have learned in years of gardening. Some I know for sure, others are still debatable. What are the ones I know for sure?

I love gardening. I love the feel of the soil in my hands. I love watching things grow and become more beautiful year after year.

I love seeing a tall tree and remembering when I planted it at eight inches high.

I love the look of a healthy, plant, well-grown and well-tended.

A good landscape design adds thousands of dollars to the value of your home and pleasure to all who see it.

Bugs don't eat much. Besides, I like the lacy look.

Vegetables and fruit from the garden taste very different from the ones in the store.

Moles go where they want. They always win, except when there's a blacksnake around.

A goldfish pond relieves stress.

Dogs and gardening don't mix, but I won't give either up.

Getting a plant from a friend makes it a living greeting card for many years.

Giving a plant to a friend is even better. You get to visit.

Grow enough for birds to eat, too, and your blood pressure will stay lower.

A hazy July day is a great time to sit on the porch, drink iced tea and watch the stars come out.

Gardeners are nice people. Everybody's a gardener in April. They're all at the nursery at the same time.

In July, only real gardeners care about it.

Watering a garden is a stress reliever. I usually get to squirt Jim at some point.

Starting a plant from scratch is amazing.

Mowing the grass makes me feel good. It looks so great when I'm done.

Building up the soil is one way to leave the world a better place.

Working in the yard is great exercise. Just do it every day and both you and your yard will look good.

The first 15 years in a place you spend planting. The next 15 you spend trimming. The last 15 you hire someone to do it. Or I probably will.

I wish my mother-in-law and my grandma could've had a greenhouse. We would've had fun there.

Happy gardening.

FALL IS THE BEST TIME TO PLANT PERENNIALS

Questions from the mail bag;

Q: I'm just now getting into gardening. I've planted a couple of perennials recently and was just wondering how late into the season planting can be done. Will plants have enough time to get established? The ones I've planted are late-blooming perennials.

A: Actually, planting can be done anytime you can get a spade into the ground to dig the hole, but the odds of a happy result vary according to the weather and the calendar. Fall - September or October - is the best time to plant perennials or trees, though. Why is that? Because in the fall, plants are growing less and that places far less demands on a root system that hasn't had time to work its way into the soil very far. The plant will concentrate on growing roots for a couple of months before a hard freeze (usually mid-October) and so will be much stronger by springtime, when growth demands are high.

Q: Is it possible to get a plant started with just a clipping? I've tried many times. I will see a plant at a friend's, get a clipping, bring it home, put it in a glass of water in the sun, and wait for roots to develop. They never do.

A: A frowny face was a good punctuation mark for this one, because it usually won't work. A few plants root in water easily, but not usually the ones we would like to plant in our yards. If they did, more people would have them.

It is a little late in the year to try this, but I suggest you try it anyway. Take several 5 or 6" tip cuttings (end of a stem) from a plant you like. Make sure you ask first. It should have leaves at the top, a second set lower, and a third set below that. Slip them into a plastic bag with a damp paper towel inside to keep them moist if you can't work with them right away. When you get home, gently snip off the pairs of leaves from the bottom two-thirds of the cutting close to the stem, leaving the top set intact, and throw what's left into a bowl of cool water as you work. You should have two to four small leaves left on the stem, and if the remaining leaves are large, cut off half of each leaf to reduce the demands for moisture. Also snip off the top of the stem to force growth to the sides.

Fix a couple of CLEAN plastic pots with NEW potting soil from the nursery, and set them in the sink in an inch or two of water to soak. Wet the bottom of the cutting where the leaves were, stick it into some rooting hormone (buy at any nursery) and tap off the excess, right where the leaves were removed. That is where the roots will develop. Get the clean pot you prepared, and use a pencil or similar item to provide holes for the stems without knocking off the hormone. Depending on the size of the pot, put a few stems in to try. In a five inch square pot, you could probably put 9 small cuttings in to develop. Remember that roots are more likely to develop near the joints of the stems. Also snip off some of ends of the top leaves to reduce need for moisture. Gently firm the soil around the stems. Put the pot near an indirect (no bright sun) source of light, and set it in a plastic dishpan or similar that can hold water and all the plants you have made. Put it near a light source, and gently drape a loose plastic bag over the top, never sealing it. The air needs to circulate, but the plastic will help hold moisture in.

Once the soil is moist, not a lot of water is required. Do NOT place this contraption in direct sunlight. That builds up heat quickly, much like it does in a car, and will quickly kill any plants unlucky enough to be inside. The goal is not to have the plants horizontal. Vertical is better.

Place it in indirect light away from a window and learn to wait - two weeks, four weeks, eight weeks - depends on the plant and the system you've set up. If one of the cuttings fails, get rid of it and the potting soil immediately. Fungus is catching.

The best time to take cuttings for many plants is early summer, after the first flush of new growth is beginning to harden off, but is not yet woody. These are called semi-soft cuttings.

I hope you have success. Even if you don't, it's fun to try. Restrain yourself from pulling those cuttings out of the soil every day to look for roots. They'll never grow if you do that. Ask me how I know this. Happy gardening!

NEGLECT EDGING ONE YEAR: GARDEN SUFFERS NEXT

Last year, in March or April, I volunteered a few hours at Dawes Arboretum in Newark, Ohio. I spent some very enjoyable time helping in the greenhouse and learned a lot about propagation.

Another day I spent on a breezy sunshiny day planting foxglove starts around Daweswood House. I asked the staff to let me know when they came in bloom. In May, I was blessed to see the end result. Surrounding the house were hundreds of foxgloves, mostly in pink and white, along with pink roses. I didn't plant them all, but the effect was breathtaking. I shall not soon forget the impact of that display.

As I planted them, I wondered how they would look, as they are not a small plant, and we planted them in beds next to the house and under low trees in the front. I needn't have worried. It was beautiful. If you are looking for ideas, take a walk or drive around Dawes. The new herb garden is beginning to mature, and interesting plants abound.

Last year, we didn't get around to edging our flower beds, and this year we are paying the price. Grass has crept into the ivy, the pachysandra, the phlox, into every bed. Jim has since rectified that on two of the beds next to the driveway, and the effect is wonderful. You don't have to have a lot of plants to show off if the beds are properly mulched and edged. A straight, deep line marks the difference between bed and lawn. It's simple to mow around, and my neatnik tendencies are assuaged instantly. (My neatnik tendencies don't extend to the house, I'm afraid.) Better yet, the grass will stop at the edge and won't pass into the bed to be hand-pulled by yours truly, until it needs to be done again.

We have tried several ways to do this chore. At one time, we purchased an edging tool. This is a long-handled tool with a flat, half-moon blade at the bottom. The blade is pushed into the ground where you want the edge to be. This part is not difficult, at least from my perspective (watching Jim do it.) It creates the edge line. Then you use a spade to remove the soil and sod from inside the line. This is the hard part. We usually end up with a couple of wheelbarrows full of sod and dirt. You can shake the dirt into the wheelbarrow and replace it into the flowerbeds or you can use sod and dirt elsewhere. With five acres of hillside, we usually have a low place that we would like to fill, so that's where ours goes. I can still tell where the spots are that we have filled over the years on the hill. The grass is thicker and greener than the other areas, and the level ground is easier to mow.

I simply throw the sod, dirt and all, into the low spot. I try to have the sod up, but layer it unmercifully. I figure the soil will eventually wash down and smother the bottom layers, and the top layer will take hold. When I'm finished, I usually see a lumpy, disorganized bunch of clumps. That's it. Gradually, the pieces level out and sink in and become level and organized. I avoid the area with the lawn mower for awhile, but eventually, I grit my teeth and just go over it. Haven't lost the mower yet. It's amazing how it settles in and looks good.

Another method we've tried is a power edger tool. We have a couple of types, both of which turn out to be a machine that does the part of the edger tool described above. In other words, the spading part still needs to be done, with just a slice mark showing. Recently, we learned of edger tools that work like very small trenchers, in that they chew out a line about an inch or two wide at the edge of the beds. This would make the work very simple, and I will be looking into renting one of these soon. I'll let you know how that goes.

But the best part is the way the lawn looks. The neatly edged mulch provides a trim to the lawn that sets it off beautifully, and makes both mulch and lawn look better.

CREATIVITY PART OF THE GARDENING PROCESS

This week, I enjoyed learning from two gardeners who didn't even know I was paying attention. I went to a friend's house to pick up something she left on her porch for me. She told me she couldn't be there, but to look around if I wanted. So when I saw the windmill and other interesting things she had about the yard, I decided to take her up on her offer.

Right beside the workshop was a medium-sized tree with a fascinating birdhouse about eye level, a boot with a bent license plate as a roof. On the side was a two-inch hole and a small dowel rod beneath it as a perch. I put my finger on the perch to see if it was solid. As I did, a small sound warned me, but I still wasn't prepared for the sudden flush of a bird exiting the hole right in front of me. Jim later said I should keep my fingers to myself, and I agreed.

Later, I found a teapot with flowers hanging on a wrought-iron pot stand and a white enamel coffee pot stuffed with plants in a flower bed. There was a small shed made of logs, with antiques nailed to its side, and scattered decoratively on the porch. A large slab of a tree stump leaned precariously to the corner.

Back at the house, I found a cozy porch with many seats, obviously a favorite spot. The porch swing held a blanket and a soft cushion with a piece of plywood on top. I wondered about that, until I saw a small foam pad by the kitchen door with a few dog treats on top. I assumed the dog treats were to encourage the use of the pad, and the plywood was to discourage the use of the swing. Those of us who love dogs can understand this completely.

A large pond was easily visible from the back of the house. This was clearly the home of someone who loves the outdoors. I left a note on a card, and wished I could stay awhile.

An email from a fellow gardener said that he had found a spot for a blue wave hydrangea under the shade of a maple tree where it would get the morning sun. His big surprise this year was the Hostas, which he had moved from the edge of the woods where they "were hardly doing anything". In the sun, the blossoms are now "trumpet-shaped and very impressive." He wants to plant a group of them at the edge of his yard. The previous owner put great store in rows of pine trees, but he is slowly overcoming that. He says he finally learned to plant things in groups. I could feel his excitement even through the email. Besides, if he loves Hydrangeas, he must be a good guy.

In my own version of creativity, it's been 14 days since I put the cuttings under the mist in the greenhouse. One hydrangea is showing healthy white roots. Others have tiny brown hairlike roots that are barely visible, and sometimes even shoot straight up from the potting soil. (I always punch them back down.) The Viburnum are showing hair-like roots also, and the leaves are a bright, healthy green. The Oakleaf hydrangeas are also showing roots, and I took them out from under the mist right away. Plants with hairy leaves like the oak leaf do not like to have water on the leaves constantly; if they do, the leaves will rot, and the plant will be lost, so I moved them to another bench without a misting system where they will stay for a week or two, and then I'll put them outside where Mother Nature can take care of them.

Even as these plants generate new life, our huge tree in the front lawn was cut down today. With a big crash, the sunshine grew much brighter at my window. The crew says that it was an Elm tree, and dying of Dutch elm disease. But Jim says the tree book verifies it as an ironwood tree. I think he is right, primarily because if that tree was an elm tree, it certainly wasn't very attractive. I can't imagine trees like that would have been mainstays in Hometown, USA, with such a straggly look.

Regardless, it is always sad to lose such an elderly part of the landscape. I hope that the young oak and maple nearby have a spurt of growth now that they're not in competition with it. When I planted those 10 years ago, I thought that someday they would replace the larger ones. I'm glad I did.

WHAT'S YOUR QUESTION?

The scientists at Ohio State University and the Licking County Extension Office regularly send me news about conditions gardeners might be interested in. For instance, Japanese beetles appeared in Ohio in mid-June to do their chewing thing. According to the scientists, we may be asking, "What DON'T Japanese Beetles eat???"

Magnesium deficiency is showing up on red maples (Acer Rubrum). Leaves may show yellowing between the veins, and young twigs show dying on the tips. Call the Extension office for more information.

Tomatoes in some areas are showing what's called "blossom end rot". This is a dark black spot on the bottom end(opposite the stem) of the ripening tomato. According to the County Extension service, it is caused by a low concentration of calcium in the soils. In my experience, it happens when not enough water has been present during the fruit's development, and if those conditions change, later fruits will not have the problem. Be patient - in Ohio the weather will change.

I called them again this week. My sister-in-law found a number of dead bats in her barn. They kept appearing a few every day for several days, and she was concerned. She knows I think bats are a good thing, as they eat many insects like mosquitoes that carry diseases. I offered to call the extension office to ask if they had heard of any problems in the area. Before I got around to it, Jim found a bat in distress on our patio. When I called them, I talked with several different persons over the course of a couple of days, and most said that it's not unusual for dead bats to be found occasionally.

But when it happens in groups, there is probably a reason. The most common reason is that insecticide has been used in quantity in the area. Since a large swampy area is below my sister-in-law's house, I assume that some state people sprayed that area for mosquitoes. The extension person said, "That's the problem with using insecticides. It affects lots of species eventually."

In more pleasant news, butterflies are beginning to grace our flowerbeds. I heard a story from one of the entomologists (bug doctor) whose neighbor mentioned how much she loved butterflies. He said, "Well, I saw you killing them two weeks ago."

She was shocked. "Me? Of course not. I love butterflies!"

"Weren't you spraying the caterpillars?" She was silent.

We all love them when they're fluttering around the flowers. But green, wiggly and munching on our beloved plants? No way.

LATE SUMMER BARGAINS AND SECRETS

If you've been planning some major garden purchases, now is the time to take a look. Many garden centers are running specials on shrubs, trees, and other perennials. Over the years, I have purchased some great shrubs in August, and some bad ones. Once I bought a dwarf rhododendron at the end of the season, at 70 percent off. I babied that thing for four years before I finally gave up and threw it away. It never did recover from a summer in a pot at the discount store parking lot. Since then, I've been a little more careful where and when I buy.

If you do buy a tree or shrub this time of year, be ready to give it lots of water and care through this growing season at least. Trim it back a little when you plant it, so it doesn't need quite as much moisture as it has been getting at the nursery, and then water weekly if it doesn't rain at least an inch. (Note: Never trim the leader or main stem of a tree unless you want a midget tree. On a shrub, you can thin out a few stems from the leader.) September and October are great times to plant trees and shrubs because the growing demands are few, and all the plant's energy can be directed to developing roots for next year. Pick a cloudy day, and don't plant too deep. Use the original soil to fill around the base, because if you give it lots of organic matter, the clay around the planting hole acts like a bathtub and holds water. You'll drown the plant eventually.

You can see the damage a lack of water does to a plant as you are driving along the freeway now. Notice the trees in the wooded areas. You will see huge number of trees that are slightly less green than the rest. If you look close, you can see leaves that are half green and half brown. These trees were damaged severely in last year's drought, and some may never recover even though we've had ample rainfall since. When your favorite shade tree starts to drop brown leaves on your lawn every week, look up and see if there is damage. One of ours is showing an entire branch in distress. I don't know if this is insect damage or drought, but it bears watching. Some trees that were damaged last year may not show signs of stress until next year, so don't discount this until a specialist tells you otherwise. Of course, if a truck rammed into it, or you built a garage next to the trunk, it could be that, too.

My plant propagation has developed into a regular monthly activity, and is showing a higher percentage of success. I'm learning. Each month since May, I make a little tour of the yard, clipping a few items from favorite shrubs at a time. These I carry immediately to the potting bench in a bucket of water, trim and treat with rooting hormone, and stick them in small pots. Under the sprinkler they go, for a couple of weeks when I can no longer stand the suspense, and I pop them out of the pot for a quick inspection for roots. Many already show these, are potted up immediately and placed back where they came from. I trim them at this time to encourage side shoots, and put them back under the sprinkler for another two weeks. By this time, they are usually hardy enough to go outside in a shady area. I have discovered two kinds of shrubs that don't like to be constantly sprinkled on the leaves. They grow for a month or so, then decline. Both have soft fuzzy leaves that don't like constant dampness. So, I move them out of the sprinkler after they are obviously developing growth, and water them by hand underneath the leaves. They are thriving under this method.

I hope you've been giving your houseplants a summer vacation outdoors. Mine get moved to the deck every summer for the humid atmosphere that they love. Please note, I never put them in direct sunlight for more than an hour or two per day. I take care to acclimate them slowly in the spring, moving them to total shade for a week or two, and very gradually, move them toward the railing where they get more sun. I bring them inside in early September after a thorough cleaning and inspection for insects.

I have a confession to make: Every one of my summer plants in containers has gone to a greater reward. I made myself a promise that I would water them daily if necessary, but they still died. I think I used potting soil that had fertilizer included, then added my own. I burned them up. The pots look great at the top off the stairs on either side, almost like pillars, but I suppose I should replace the brown plants.

A neighbor found a source of free horse manure and piled it deeply on his vegetable garden early this spring. He said it was well rotted, but I doubted it. Rotted horse manure to a farmer is not the same as to a gardener. Of course, his plants started to burn. He said he had nothing to lose at that point, so he added some lime. The garden has recovered and is doing beautifully. Maybe I should have tried that on my containers.

I planted some moonflower vines this spring, and gave many away to friends. My most successful one is about four feet tall right now, but a friend told me his wife's vine is up to the top of their archway trellis, and across the top. I asked what her secret was. He said she just put a little Miracle Gro on it when she planted it. Now there's a secret. The only problem is I took away my fertilizer license long ago, like I took away my husband's bleach license in the laundry room. We're both dangerous with chemicals.

GARDENING GOOD FOR SOUL, HEALTH AND EARTH

I bumped into two people last week who told me about their water gardens. One friend had spent last spring recuperating from health problems and often sat for an hour or two on her patio whenever she felt sick. She found herself thinking about what she could do to improve it, and finally settled on a water garden at one corner and flowerbeds around the rest. She is much better now, and her husband built her what she dreamed of for the patio. They invited us over to see it. She had some floating hyacinths and a flowering bog plant that I was unfamiliar with. Her husband had lugged many stones to line the flower beds with, and all was beautiful and new. She said she only wished they had gotten a larger one. I realized I had heard that many times. Her husband said she'd have to get someone else to build the next one. Jim laughed. He's built two for the same reason.

She doesn't have any fish yet. I was interested to see that her pond has been in for six weeks, and it was as clear as if it had just been filled. I was surprised that no algae bloom had started, nor that any algae growth was visible on the walls of the hard plastic pond. I think it's because the pond is in a shaded area under a tree. We explained the winter procedure to them and cautioned them about breaking ice with a hammer. A friend of mine lost many large koi fish from the concussion it caused in the water. You can gently make a hole in the ice with a heated pot of water, just setting it on the ice to slowly melt it. Better still, you can purchase a stock tank de-icer and just plug it in when cold weather comes and remove it in the spring. Keeping a hole in the ice is critical to allow oxygen to enter into the water, and carbon dioxide to exit. As waste from the plants and fish decays, a gas is produced that is toxic to the hibernating fish and frogs. Leaving a solid ice layer will kill most of the fish. I can hear you saying that they make it fine in the wild. True, but usually there is an opening somewhere due to springs or currents. Ponds don't have those.

We told her that you can buy or order frogs, tadpoles, and snails each year. We had learned to wait until spring to clean the pond so that the frogs and snails have some mud at the bottom of the pond where they can winter over. This way, they will reproduce every year. Frogs, snails and tadpoles all help keep the pond clean by eating insects and algae.

Both of them instinctively knew this garden was important for her, before it was built and after. What a beautiful way to think on positive things while life gives you a tumble - build a garden. Now they go outside to sit and listen to the water bubbling, bubbling.

Other good news from the country came in the form of the most beautiful clear honey we've ever seen. Jim is strutting around like a new father, telling everyone he sees about how his bees produced it. We knew not to heat it this year, and we had some frames of comb honey, which Jim loves. We expect to get more from the same hive by fall, provided Jim can leave the poor bees alone long enough to make it. He loves to go up and "check on the bees". Usually they're very placid, but I think they're saying, "Would you please let us bee?"

One hive has not produced well, and we got a new queen bee last month to replace the old one. For some reason, she was not doing well, and if the queen is off stride, so goes the hive. Just like our house. They will need the rest of the summer to create enough for themselves to get through the winter.

It may be my imagination, but it seems as if my garden is producing better, and my flowers blooming more often since we got the bees. Every gardener should consider housing bees for this reason. Bees in the wild have been pretty much decimated by the mites that attack them. For this reason, unless a beekeeper in your area provides them, you probably won't be stepping on them in your grass like you used to when you were a kid running barefoot.

We have begun to harvest peas, asparagus, lettuce, onions, garlic, radishes, broccoli, and spinach from our garden. Squash is begging to overwhelm us already, though I love it. I'll probably have to think of ways to hide it in the meals, because everyone else is tired of it already. Our cucumbers didn't make it, probably because of too much rain. Jim's favorite garden meal is cucumber and tomato salad, so we'll have to rely on neighbors or the grocery to provide them this year. Recently we planted two shrubs I grew in the greenhouse. One is a beautiful leafed Viburnum, and the other a blue wave Hydrangea. I gave these both away as fast as I could get them to mature, so I decided to plant other ones for cuttings. People love the blue flowers - and so do I. Both of these are very easy to start, and make me feel like a real gardener. So I keep doing them. Whatever gardening you enjoy, keep doing it. It's good for the world, your family, and for you.

AUGUST: MONTH OF TRANSITIONS

August is a great transition month. While the Dog Days of summer bear down, the dry weather slows the growth of the lawn and the weeds in the flower garden. Since the tomatoes aren't overwhelming us yet, it's a great time to plan for improving the landscape.

One thing you're very aware of now is the need for watering equipment. Ease of use is key to helping motivate you to do it. A built-in irrigation system is top-of-the-line, but you can imitate the convenience with a do-it-yourself system available at many garden centers and home remodeling centers. These systems use black plastic tubing that can be tailored to your specific layout and plants, or to general areas. Timers complete the system, and depending on the type, can be set to water automatically once a week or every day for a specified length of time. They can also be as simple as a windup timer that shuts off when it unwinds.

Of course, it's seldom necessary to water every day, and you can seriously weaken many plants, including lawns, by watering too much or too frequently. Over-watered plants often exhibit similar symptoms to under-watered plants: pale, spindly growth and leaves.

Unless you want a magazine quality lawn, watering sparingly is sufficient. We have had several helpful rains, even during the hot spells, and usually that's enough. In a way, lawns have a built-in safety valve. They turn brown to conserve moisture. Does this mean they are dead? No - just waiting for the next rain. So don't panic if your lawn is turning brown right now. Just wait for Mother Nature to do what she always does - come around again.

From the totally automatic system down to a hose with a nozzle, you have a myriad of choices. I have purchased two or three timers to place at various faucets. I take a hose up to these, and place them with a sprinkler at the spot I want to water. Then I set the timer for ten to fifteen minutes and go read a book. (Or write a column). When the timer shuts off, I move the sprinkler to the next spot.

If you don't have a timer, you can get the same effect by running out to the sprinkler and moving it. This has the added effect of dousing you with cool water much more cheaply than installing a swimming pool.

When is it most important to water? When you've planted a new shrub or tree. These are under great stress from the move, and need a lot of help. Long soakings a couple of times a week are not excessive, especially in August. The best time to plant trees and shrubs is in September, because the temperature has cooled, growth demand on the plant is very low, fall rains are coming soon, and plants have time to develop lots of roots before a hard frost.

So, before the tomatoes come on, look into a watering system. It's always fun to "accidentally" spray your spouse too. Just don't mention my name.

IT'S JULY - JUST ENJOY YOUR GARDEN!

I love gardening in July. Even though it's hot and dry, most of our plants survive and even thrive. They've been doing it for centuries without our help. Plants that are already weak or very young may not make it, but there's always another year.

This week, I enjoyed some special things from my garden. The first tomato is always a treat. This one was small, bright red, hiding near the bottom of the tomato plant. My husband brought it in and carefully cut it into quarters. We ate them slowly, so as to savor its flavor. My first question was, "Which kind is this?" You may remember that I planted several heirloom varieties this year. This one had no tag but I can tell you it was delicious! Ah, well.

The second thing I enjoyed was a bouquet of gold and blue flowers now sitting on my coffee table. I used to be reluctant to cut those beautiful flowers and bring them in. Eventually, I realized that cutting them often stimulates the plant to produce new flowers, much like pruning spurs new growth.

So now I cut them without guilt, and put them in pitchers, vases, jars, anything handy. They never fail to bring a smile as I pass by. I know nothing of flower arranging, but how can something so beautiful look otherwise just because they're in a bunch?

The best thing from my garden this week was fresh blueberries. Unlike the tomato, these are first-come, first-serve. I just discovered that our berry bushes bear a lot more than I've been led to believe.

I've watched my husband pull berries from the bush as he passes by many times this week. These are particularly tasty, because they are from bushes that never bore before. The shrubs have been there quite some time, but were planted in an area much too shady for them to bear fruit.

This year, however, we removed some trees to install the greenhouse, and voila! The bushes are loaded. There's nothing quite so sweet as berries straight from the bush or vine.

As I am pondering which plants to "pot up," (greenhouse lingo for move to bigger pots), I casually stroll over to the blueberries and enjoy a treat.

July is the time I really enjoy my garden. It's too hot to work hard, too late to plant early, and too early to plant late (at least I tell myself this). So I usually walk around just to enjoy the flower beds.

As I do, sometimes weeds call to me, and I cannot pass by without pulling the most obvious ones. It doesn't take many trips of pulling five or ten weeds to keep those beds beautiful, especially when I pull them before they get very large.

Other things I enjoyed this week were the new plants I started over the last year from cuttings or seeds. I moved them outside to a nursery bed, and placed a sprinkler over them. Most of them I potted up to a bigger container, and added a small amount of slow-release fertilizer. I think they must be happy, because they have responded by producing new leaves and turning a bright healthy green. Drops of water sparkle on their leaves in the dappled sunshine beneath the trees. I celebrate each new leaf like a parent does a new tooth. The pots include maple, oak, and buckeye trees, hydrangeas, hollies, boxwood, coneflowers, Stella D'oros, miscanthus and fountain grass.

Some of these I am growing for relatives and friends, some for me, some for an experiment, and some just for the joy of growing. There's always a spot or a friend that would enjoy a plant.

AMERICA'S FOUNDING GARDENERS

Gardeners are optimists. They look at a patch of dirt and see the beauty of possibility. They throw themselves into the task with shovel and mattock, cleaning out the rocks and weeds, making the situation right for growth.

Gardeners believe in the future. They plant a tree when they probably won't enjoy its shade. They know that someone else will sit beneath it, drinking a glass of iced tea, thankful for its beauty and shelter.

We celebrate the birth of our country this week, and it's time to rest for a while to be thankful for what we have. Even George Washington took time off from his garden to celebrate the Fourth of July.

We live in a nation where we are free to express our beliefs, to worship as we wish, where our rights are protected zealously from rampant government or oppression. We don't call our President "Your Highness" - we call him Mister. Our Founding Fathers wanted it that way.

At least two of our founding Fathers were gardeners. George Washington, father of our nation, loved his Mount Vernon. A diary entry on Thursday, April 3d, 1760, shows his attention to planting conditions: "Sowd my Fallow Field in Oats today and harrow them in viz 10 1/2 bushels. Got done about three o'clock. Got several Composts and laid them to dry in order to mix with the Earth from the field below to try their several Virtues." A man so attentive to the earth could not fail to care for a nation.

Thomas Jefferson wrote many of the words that guide America today. A visit to his hilltop home, Monticello, confirms his love of plants. The grounds have been restored to his original design by using his garden and farm journals, which he kept in detail. The gardens today contain vegetables, fruits, flowers, and shrubs in tightly organized beds. From the scarlet runner beans to the grape arbors, to the fishpond, the visitor gets a sense of order amidst bounty - a blessing our nation also enjoys, thanks to Jefferson.

In a letter written on his last day in office, President Washington wrote, "If our experiment in freedom succeeds, the people themselves will hold the ultimate authority in our new land...all the sacrifices made to win the struggle for freedom (will) not be wasted or lost. I (can) feel assured that come what may - whether it be political bickering, jealousies, intrigue or any other evil natural in a government where free and God-loving men express their opinions - when all is said and done, our country rests in good hands, in those of its people."

A true leader - and a true gardener - respects his or her creation.

HAPPY BIRTHDAY, USA!

Even George Washington took time off from his garden to celebrate the Fourth of July, so I'm going to do the same.

I love this country. Our nation has spawned the likes of Abraham Lincoln, Martin Luther King Jr., Madelyn Murray O'Hare, and the 90 year-old veterans who proudly salute the flag in the Fourth of July parade.

From the factory worker, to the retailers, to the farmers, teachers, and the United Way, the American spring is alive. When the great sleeping tiger of the American public is aroused, things happen. We have seen a peaceful transfer of power, even in scandal, as our Founding Fathers planned. Our people fight battles, disease and ideas with strength, courage, and words.

Our ancestors had a spirit of adventure to come here. We were a frontier, untested waters, and they came anyway. They left their home and their families to start a new life. This is the stock from which we come.

You can see it: a strength, a willingness to risk all for a good cause. You can see it on the playing fields and in Congress. You can see it in our children, our elderly, and our homes. We have a tradition of freedom and responsibility that runs deep and accomplishes much.

We live in a nation where our forefathers thoughtfully decided to call our President "Mister" rather than "Your Highness". Our White House is small and simple compared to the palaces of the world. They wanted it that way.

In our nation, reporters can disturb a President before breakfast. We can say what we think about this government without fear of imprisonment or reprisal, and without staring down tanks on the Courthouse Square. What a privilege this is! We can choose who we want to lead us. We can make a difference.

We are blessed. Remember that when you see the flag pass by this Fourth of July.

GARDEN POND SOURCE
OF ENJOYMENT

I always wanted to live by the water, and now I do. Granted it's not the Atlantic Ocean, or even Buckeye Ocean (Buckeye Lake for you foreigners), but it's almost as good. It's my very own water garden, complete with koi, water lilies, and bullfrogs. The frogs came on their own.

There's nothing quite as relaxing as the sound of splashing water. And the plants in this garden don't wilt in the heat! It doesn't have to be mowed, or weeded. It's less work than a lawn.

Building it wasn't difficult. (Of course, Jim did all the digging.) Nor was it difficult to add the water plants and the fish. We were thrilled when the first frogs showed up. Soon I took to enjoying my morning coffee by the pond. One morning, I must've startled the frog, because he jumped right past my head.

Once a friend stopped by with her two children for a visit. As I showed her around my greenhouse 100 yards away, her son stayed by the pond. Suddenly, I heard a loud, "Hey!" She looked at me, startled, thinking he might be hurt or had done something wrong. I laughed. I said, "I think he found the frog." The next words from her son were, "Is that a REAL frog?"

I assured him it was. By the time we got over to the pond, he had discovered that the frog would allow him to rub his back. Learning of this, my husband delighted in demonstrating it to anyone who would watch. But it took Seth to start the tradition.

We began to notice new varieties of birds visiting our feeders, apparently drawn by the water. But the fish are the best part. Feeding them is a treat I often share with guests, and Queenie, my favorite one, will eat from my hand. If we have guests for dinner, sometimes I float candles in the water. Yes - you can buy candles that float. The fish, curious, come up and poke at the candles, sloshing water on them and dousing the flames.

The first summer, I noticed the fish behaving strangely. They madly dashed around the pond, burrowing into the roots of the floating plants, and even coming half out of the water at times. This went on for a couple of weeks, and it wasn't long before I noticed a tiny glint of light between the lily pads. It was a baby fish, so small it was very difficult to see. I shouted for my husband to come see. This is now an annual occurence. By the way, anybody need some baby Koi?

When we first installed the water garden, we chose a small pre-formed plastic one, which quickly proved to be inadequate. A stray cat was able to grab my prized Koi fish out of the pond because he had no deep place to escape. So we dug a deeper hole and bought a flexible liner rather than the molded one. This larger pond gave the fish and plants more room and depth to roam. Not huge, but good. Soon, I discovered that the koi had been a voracious feeder, and once mine was gone, plants grew quickly.

About this same time, I took off the fountain sprayer and allowed the water to just gurgle out of the pump. Suddenly the water lilies were much happier without the constant drenching, and they responded by doubling in size. All of this plant growth increased the shade and decreased the carbon dioxide in the water, and the algae disappeared!

The filter could now handle the rest, and the pond was beautifully clear. We still have algae "blooms" every spring and during very hot weather, but I just see it as part of the process.

Yes, the fish stay in the pond all winter, and have for five years now. We just float a stock tank de-icer in the pond to keep a hole in the ice for oxygen, and the fish and frogs hibernate at the bottom during the coldest months. A friend of mine used a hammer to break the ice for oxygen, and the shock killed all her fish, so don't try that.

We've had many inches of ice on top, and never lost a fish in winter. My dog likes to jump up on the ice to get a drink of water in the opening, but she hasn't broken through yet. We made some mistakes along the way, but you can probably tell that the pond is still my favorite part of the garden.

KEEP WATERING DURING DRY SPELL

My garden is struggling. I hope that by the time you read this, we've received a drenching rain, and the grass is so high that everyone in the neighborhood is mowing his/her lawn at the same time. Noisy, but satisfying.

My son once worked for a local golf course as a greenskeeper. He took great pride in, as he put it, "doing things that golfers would like." He loved to play golf.

One summer when he worked there, it was 100 degrees many days. One day he called home to say that he and his friend Robert were the only ones playing on the golf course that afternoon. "Imagine that," I mumbled, thinking this must be his father's genes talking.

One of his jobs there was to water the greens. He spent many hours lugging equipment around the entire course, setting up sprinklers to keep the greens as healthy as possible. He told me, "Mom, just a little rain is so much better than hours of sprinkling."

I can attest to that. I wonder where all that water goes? I've been using sprinkling systems and hoses much more than I used to, and I really can't see much improvement in the plants. I guess if they're still living, that's an improvement

One thing I've never done is water our lawn. I figure if it gets brown, so be it. It'll come back later. Landscape plants are another matter. Established plants are not usually threatened by the heat, unless it is severe and prolonged. However, new plants are extremely threatened and need to be closely cared for if you like them at all, and hope they'll be back next year.

Young trees especially need extra water the entire first year while they are developing a root system. Don't expect to see a lot of growth on any new plant, because underneath is where the action is the first year. An old saying about perennials is this: The first year, they sleep; the second year, they creep; the third year, they leap! This means that they take their sweet time to do much growing, at least where it can be seen by the gardener and his or her neighbors. They plan their operation by developing their support systems, logistics and line of attack before they put on the public show. (A lesson that soldiers and community leaders would do well to emulate.)

But I digress. I try to conserve water, even though we have our own well, so I don't water needlessly. I do water to protect stressed plants, new plants, and the vegetable garden. That mulch we put on two months ago is helping tremendously to conserve any remaining moisture in the soil where we need it, but it can't do it alone.

Once when we were in a severe drought, I started collecting rinse water from my clothes washer into a plastic trash container with wheels. I figured the rinse water would have the least soap and other chemicals in it to harm the plants. I would move the hose over to the container after the wash cycle was finished. Then we would roll this out to the plants and gently dip the water onto the plants. I don't know how much this helped the plants, but it made me feel a lot better.

For now, we are using a mixture of sprinkling hoses, soaker hoses, and sprinklers, along with an assortment of faucet splitters and spray nozzles. Has anyone out there ever figured out how to set one of those jiggly things that you stick in the ground? I usually back away and let Jim have a go at it.

I try to water each area every two or three days for a half hour or so in this heat, and a different area every day. This is not enough to keep the plants going strong, but I don't expect it to be. I only expect to keep them alive until the weather breaks.

We used to collect rain in a barrel at the downspout, and allow it to leak out through a soaker hose up close to the house where rain seldom reaches. I gave this up when I realized that algae and who knows what grew in that tube and eventually went on my plants. I didn't think this was healthy, especially for new plantings.

A LADY IN WAITING

What's your favorite part of gardening? Bringing in a beautiful bouquet for the dinner table? Growing your dinner in your own vegetable patch? Coming from work and catching the first glimpse of your well-manicured lawn?

All of those are special, I admit. But my favorite part is creating new plants by propagation. My mother-in-law used to start roses from cuttings. She brought home cut roses from bouquets at work at a local inn, and scattered them about her lawn under gallon jugs weighed down by bricks. These served as mini-greenhouses for her adopted plants. It seemed like alchemy to me, but under her care, they flourished. A word of caution: On a hot day, it the gallon jug is weighted down, the heat can build up quickly and "roast" the plant. Taking a small rock to tip the jar open a little at the bottom helps protect the plant.

You too can do it, and your thumb can stay the normal color. June is a great time to try, for plants have just started their new, soft growth perfect for making new plants.

Here's how: Go out in your yard (or ask a friend) and look for a shrub you like. Hydrangeas work very well. Snip off a few ends of branches to a length of 4-6", and throw them immediately into a bucket of water. This will not harm the shrub. Prepare a pot with potting soil and vermiculite or sand (not dirt from the garden), and water it well.

To "make" the cutting, you remove the leaves on the lower two-thirds of the stem, leaving only a couple of leaves at the top. If the leaves are large, cut off or tear off about half of each leaf, so as not to demand too much moisture to support them while they are developing roots. The leaf nodes (where the leaves join the stem) are where the roots will develop, so trim the stem just under the bottom node. Make sure there are no leaves still attached at that point. Wet the bottom of the stem, and stick it into a small bottle of powdered rooting hormone, available any place where they sell plants. Gently tap off the excess powder.

In the pot you have chosen and filled with potting soil, make some planting holes with a stick or pencil. You're going to crowd the pot with cuttings to help them support each other, and to increase the humidity in the pot. Place about 9 cuttings in a 4" pot. Put a cutting in each hole, and gently firm the soil around it. Keep the rest of the cuttings in water until their turn to be planted.

When they are all planted, mist the leaves with a gentle spray, and insert two sticks into the pot as support. Place a clear plastic bag loosely over this support, large enough so that it doesn't touch the plants, and loose enough so that there is air circulation. Sealing things will help mold to develop and kill your new plants. Do not tie or attach the plastic at the bottom, or the plants will probably not survive. Place the pot away from direct sunlight, and keep it moist but not standing in water or soggy.

Eventually, depending on which plant you chose, you will see new leaves begin to appear. Though this is heartening, it does not necessarily mean that roots have developed. Plants have a desire to survive, and leaves help them create food for themselves. Without roots developing, they will soon wither. Resist the temptation to poke your finger in to find the roots. Call a friend to help distract you. Chew gum. (This works for quitting smoking, too.) Use the weed whacker outside. Anything. Just don't bother those cuttings for a few more days.

When you're content that the plant is healthy and growing, you can test for roots by gently tugging at the plant. If it resists, it has probably developed roots. This usually occurs two to four weeks after sticking the cuttings, depending on the plant. Some actually take months. If roots have developed, it is time to move the baby plant to a home of its own, a process called "potting on". You can use a small scoop or tablespoon to take out each rooted plant with roots intact and move it to its own pot. Put these pots back in the same sheltered location for another week or two to adjust, and then gradually acclimate them to outdoor weather. They will need to be coddled awhile longer (much as we send money to kids in college). A year or two of growth will usually make them ready to be placed in a permanent outdoor spot. Some plants require more time to grow to the size you see in nurseries. CAUTION: I actually spend more for plants at the nursery now than I did before I learned the art of propagating cuttings, perhaps because I can appreciate the skill, care, and time it takes to grow a good plant. However, you really can have landscape plants for free - if you're better at waiting than I am.

KIDS AND PLANTS GO TOGETHER

When you are choosing plants for this year's garden, don't forget your kids and grandkids. Choose some fun things to catch their interest. I first realized the power of this years ago, when one of the kids next door got a birthday card. Inside was a small cellophane bag with four large seeds, and instructions to plant them and see what came up. Later I saw him out along the fence in the back yard with his mother, digging up a small semicircle of earth next to a fence post.

Of course, every day he raced out to see if anything was growing. He was thrilled when some green poked through. (I can relate to that.) Those plants grew so fast it was amazing. Very quickly they were taller than the boy who planted them. You've probably already guessed that they were sunflowers.

He was really proud of those giant flowers and showed them to everyone who would take the time to look. A lot of enjoyment, and hopefully a lifelong love of gardening, came from those four seeds.

Giving children their own space, tools, and crops is a great way to get them involved in gardening and away from the TV. Your kids might enjoy, for example, planting a potato, spaghetti squash, peanuts, corn, pumpkins, watermelons, strawberries, popcorn, or anything they like to eat from the garden.

Other plants can be fun, too, but choose ones that are easy to grow, like marigolds or cosmos, or enjoyable to touch like lamb's ears (soft and fuzzy) or just plain interesting like a sensitive plant (these collapse when you touch them.) My mother-in-law used to love to get someone to touch one, and then when it folded, shout "You killed it!" (Relax. They come back quickly.)

Another great choice is a moonflower vine. These grow very quickly in their one season, and give giant white flowers (like a moon) that bloom at sunset. Imagine the fun watching the moonflowers open on a hot summer night.

Another idea was to create a children's garden above ground, using landscape timbers in a square. Dig out the sod first, then lay the timbers on top of the ground in a square shape, attaching them at the corners. (You'll have to ask my husband how to do that!) Fill with any good topsoil or mixture of garden soil, peat moss, and/or compost. Mix thoroughly, add kids, seeds, and stand back. Give them a watering can, a small scoop, and a little supervision.

Remember though, that these raised planters dry out much faster than plants in the ground, so they will need to be watered more often.

Don't insist the rows be straight. Whoever said plants had to be in rows, anyway? Probably the same person who used to make me color inside the lines. Let them be creative. Of course, five plants within a one-inch square won't work, but that's part of the learning too.

Giving a child a couple of tools of their very own might be a good investment. You can get brightly colored tools that they would enjoy. Don't forget to give them a place to store them, too.

Can you see the many lessons that can be learned from a garden project? But the kids shouldn't know that. They should just think it's fun.

For the finishing touch, help them paint a sign, "Megan's Garden", or "Jason's Spot", attach it to a tomato stake, and put it in the middle of their garden.

PLANT A SHADY FUTURE

Since it's been so hot, I've been spending a lot of time in shade lately. (Actually in air conditioning, but this is what you call poetic license.) What I have learned is that there are some very beautiful plants that grow in shade - in fact, they demand it.

Ever take a walk in the woods, and inhale deeply that musky, damp, earthy smell? That's the aura of shade-loving plants, and a healthy eco-system that knows how to sustain itself, without any help from us - can you imagine? NO fertilizer, insecticide, pesticide, herbicide, any of those cides. Just Mother Nature.

A friend recently asked me about adding flower beds to her yard. She said that the only problem was that she really didn't have any space for them. She quickly added, "At least without taking out some trees, and you can't really grow anything in the shade, can you?"

I said, "You sure can." I didn't add that my favorite garden spot (next to my water garden and my greenhouse) is my shade garden.

I stumbled on the concept years ago at Ohio State University. It was a very hot summer, and I had to wait for my husband at the Agriculture building during some appointments. Outside was a shady area, and I wandered in. In the deepest shade, under some huge trees, and under some small ornamental trees, sat an inviting bench. The landscaper invited me in.

I took the offer and sat down. It was much cooler than by the hot parking lot. It was noticeably quieter, too. The soil was bare under the bench, a testament to many feet having traveled there. The trees around me were obviously happy, though the smaller ones were not as full as they might have been out under the sun on their own.

Under them were more plants that eventually drew me out of my seat to investigate closer. There were many Hostas, of course, a plant that I had just come to know. These were huge and had spread far. There were other shrubs and ground covers, some with flowers, others with leaves of all shapes and colors.

I followed the path away from the building. As I walked, the plants became less mature and the shade less deep. Apparently, horticulture students added to the garden every year, and I had been sitting in the original one. About a half mile away, the garden became very sunny, formal and modern.

I enjoyed that too, but my mind went back to the peace of the first garden. I went back and found the horticulture library in the building. A book on shade gardens kept me busy while I waited. I wrote down the Latin names for the plant I liked, and went home with ideas of my own shade garden.

I picked out a spot by the road underneath several trees. We mulched heavily, and planted a hosta or two that fall. The ground was not conducive that year to a woodland garden, but I could see its future. Next spring, we added a few plants and more mulch. We had to dig through hard earth and roots still.

When we had guests, I would say, "Would you like to see my shade garden?" They would say yes, politely. We'd stroll down to the garden, and they would look. When I looked I saw that garden around the bench at Ohio State. When they looked, they saw a few straggly plants. Eventually I learned that I shouldn't show it to people until it was more mature.

It's several years later, and on these hot days, I often gaze out from my air conditioning to those huge hostas silhouetted against the hot sun. The ground covers now cover most of the bed. They include Sweet Woodruff, a fast spreader, a polkadot plant with both blue and pink flowers simultaneously, and another ground cover almost like a philodendron whose name escapes me.

Other plants are liriope, ferns, and European Ginger. I hoped the ginger would spread, but the rate it's going, I'll be in the ground before it covers a square foot. That is my official shade garden, but I have other shady garden areas. One is covered by pachysandra under the trees, another under the pines with three of my favorite shrubs, hydrangeas. These have survived the hot summers and wet springs with panache, but haven't gotten very large because I keep raiding them for cuttings to start new ones.

A wooded area behind our house is so shaded that a couple of mowings per summer keeps it beautiful. Nothing I could plant or arrange would come close to this natural woodland. We put some ivy and myrtle starts there this year, and basically ignored them during this heat wave.

My husband tells me they are still surviving. (I'm in the air conditioning, remember?) A few years from now, I hope to enjoy looking at them from my window on a bright snowy day. As I told my friend, shady gardens are one of my favorites.

JUNE THE MONTH OF NEW CREATIONS

Birds know it. Shrubs know it. Gophers know it. Graduates know it. Pastors know it. June is a month of beginnings. When else are new things created? OK, lots of other times. But June is, well, special. So many brides walk down the aisle to their new life, and seniors to theirs, that you can't help but be excited in June.

For a gardener, this is the month of new creations as well. Shrubs and perennials have sent new soft growth out for a month or more, and their tissue is at a delicate crossroads. It is no longer brand new. It is beginning to gain strength, like those brides and graduates, to harden off to a point where a new life is possible. OK, maybe a little too eloquent.

In other words, in terms of cuttings, we are moving from the softwood stage to the semi-softwood stage. June is a great time to take cuttings! This morning I was working in my greenhouse and was thrilled to see that the viburnum cuttings I took about one month ago have developed roots. Or half of them at least. This is after many failed attempts at different times of the year. This plant gets woody earlier than most, so apparently, May is a better for its propagation. I never cease to be gratified when I see those white, healthy roots clinging to a ball of soil, where only weeks before was a green stem.

Try it. It's not hard. Take a clean knife or pruning shears or scissors outside with a small container of water. Find a shrub or plant that wouldn't be harmed by losing a stem or two and cut the tips of some stems to a length of 4 to 6 inches. Choose a non-woody plant. Cut directly below a leaf joint, or node. Throw the cutting immediately into the water. Take several cuttings the same way. Four or five will do.

Take these to a bench or table outdoors, and gather a medium-sized pot, some potting soil or plain vermiculite, a sprinkling can of water, and some rooting hormone. Rooting hormone is available at any nursery or plant center, and is important to the process. You can do it without, but are much more likely to have problems, so why not use it? Success is a lot more fun than failure. Ask me how I know this.

Put the rooting medium (potting soil or vermiculite) into the pot and moisten it thoroughly. Let it drain while you "make" the cuttings. You can cut or pull leaves from the bottom of the cutting about two-thirds of the way up. You should have two leaves at top, and another group of leaves below, with the cut stem a couple of inches further down.

If the leaves are large, cut them in half. Why, you say? Too many or too large leaves demand too much moisture to survive, and without roots, the cutting is unable to supply this. Removing several leaves, and reducing the size of large ones helps to reduce the amount of moisture needed to keep the cutting alive until roots develop.

When you pull off leaves, sometimes some of the side will peel off with them. This is not a problem, and this "wounding" is even a good thing, as it exposes more of the plant's natural hormones to the soil and increases the possibility developing there. But be gentle.

Now you can use your rooting hormone according to directions. Use your stick (not the cutting) to make a hole in the potting soil or vermiculite, and insert the cutting. Gently press the material around the stem. You can put nine cuttings into one 3 to 4 inches pot.

Now insert two sticks into the sides of the pots, so that the ends are a couple of inches higher than the cuttings. Over this, you will place a clear plastic bag, like a freezer bag. The bottom should hang loosely below the top of the pot, so that air can move up and down, but the plants are protected from drafts, and humidity is trapped inside. If you seal it tight, you will probably grow more mold than plants. Ask me how I know this.

The rest is entertainment. Watch the plant daily, and you hopefully can see it getting happier and happier. New leaves means it's time to remove the bag and dream of the future plant in your yard. Leave it in a protected area for a month or two longer before planting to ensure strong root growth. Pat yourself on the back for saving a few dollars and creating a new plant, or several.

Addicting, isn't it?

KITCHEN GARDEN FEEDS BODY, SOUL AND WILDLIFE

If you like to cook or eat from an herb and kitchen garden, it is an excellent addition to your backyard. The closer to your kitchen, the more likely you are to dash out for that last-minute garnish for your steak or vegetable salad. Mine is in full view of my kitchen windows, and invariably, as we're ready to sit down to a meal, Jim says, "want me to bring in some _____?" So, our dinners become lukewarm as he picks something to go with.

For several weeks now, we have enjoyed lettuce, onions, asparagus, and spinach. Peas, carrots and radishes are almost ready. Local rabbits are getting more broccoli than we are and have started on our newly planted raspberries, too.

In our kitchen garden, the queen is always the tomato. Nothing is used more. Jim eats the first ones while standing between the rows in early August. The next ones accompany our meals as shiny bright circles on our plates or decorate salads nightly. The last are brought inside in huge buckets and pressed to a thick rolling boil in large pots, amid steamy windows and stacks of basil and fennel. Eventually, these are poured into clean glass jars, labeled, and stacked in rows in the pantry. Each and every time I use them, I remember the tall vines sagging with the bright red fruits, feel a little smug about the effort it took, and am proud of a job well done.

It was in canning tomatoes that I first realized the benefits of using fresh spices. Dumped into an 8-quart of thickening tomato sauce, my own homegrown basil and thyme added a fragrance to my sauce and my home that no dried spice could match. I've been hooked on herbs ever since.

So, I have carefully added herbs to my flower garden. I say carefully because I once planted mint there, and spent 10 years getting rid of it. Chives, too, though masquerading as a ladylike and cooperative plant, managed to spread via the seeds produced by those innocent lavender flowers. I'm still pulling chivies out of my pansies and mums.

Other herbs, while not invasive, can be somewhat rangy and unattractive, so I have limited mine to ones that are more disciplined. Thyme, for example, is a creeping perennial that comes in many attractive varieties, smells wonderful and can be added to many foods.

Our favorite herb by far is rosemary. I grow this in pots so I can move it into the greenhouse each fall. Of course, you could plant it each spring if you'd rather. We use rosemary on chicken, steak, pork, and tomato dishes.

In other news, as they say on TV, you may have noticed hordes of slimy brown things on your plants outdoors, on the bottom of your pots, or holes appearing on your landscape plants each morning. The slugs love this warm wet weather and are thriving. You can buy controls for them at the plant centers, or you can sprinkle salt on them one by one (this helps to relieve aggression - yours of course), or you can wait till they go away.

Finally, if you haven't already, it's a good time to pinch back (cut out the tips of) any mums that are coming back from last year. This will promote bushiness and give you lots of bragging rights this fall.

GARDENER LESSONS FROM THE BEES

This week I'm doing a birds and bees talk. I knew that would get your attention. You might want to lay a book across this article in case your children come into the room.

We have a new hobby. We needed one - we haven't had a new one for a year or two and money was beginning to pile up in the corner. You know how it is.

So Jim went off to bee school, called the Licking County Bee Inspector three or four times a day for advice and eventually became the proud owner of a hive of bees. These bees were the gentle kind, we were told. They only sting bee inspectors.

So we put them in the field in full view of the house where Jim could bother them constantly. He feeds them, waters them, medicates them and generally hovers over them as if they couldn't survive without him. Me he forgets in the kitchen.

Did I know, he asks, that bees in the wild are being decimated by a parasitic mite? Apparently, our fruit and nut production are dependent on good old-fashioned beekeeping to provide bees to pollinate their stamens. Or is it pistils? I can never remember.

I thought that this was quite an amusing hobby for my husband until I saw on my Master Gardener class schedule a session on bees. I asked the long-time beekeeper, Jim Wall, what benefit bees were to gardeners.

"Did you ever see an apple that's well-developed on one side, and disfigured on the other?" he asked.

Why do men always answer a question with another question?

"Yes."

"Well, that's probably because it was only pollinated on one side."

Bees are terrific, loyal pollinators, according to Mr. Wall. Some plants cannot self-pollinate, and rely totally on insect pollination.

My next lesson about bees was with Charla Devine of Devine Farms, who raises pumpkins. "No bees, no pumpkins," Ms. Devine told me. This is a lady who speaks straight.

Once our bees were beginning to be comfortable in their new home, Jim and I noticed them on a warm spring evening on our viburnum shrub. This has a heavily scented flower that attracts bees and sister-in-law alike when it's in bloom. We watched as the bees busily visited every flower, tracking pollen with them from one to another. Once came out from deep in the bush with yellow saddlebags on each leg. This is how they carry the pollen back to the hive. It was very peaceful watching them. All seemed right with the world.

The bees worked feverishly as nectar began to come in, and the hive quickly regenerated itself. Jim's courage was increasing exponentially at the same time, so much so that one day he left his Superman-style bee jacket and netted helmet hanging on a hook in the garage while he went to check on the bees.

"What on earth is wrong with your face?" I asked him.

The next morning he bundled off for a doctor's opinion on how he could give a speech that day without looking like a buffalo. Doc charged him $30, pronounced him healthy, and wondered if he'd have any extra comb honey this year.

The Bee Inspector said Jim got stung because the bees didn't recognize him without his helmet.

CONTESTANTS TEACH JUDGES

Last week I had the pleasure of serving as one of the judges for the Advocate's Garden contest. We drove over a fourth of the county, uphill and down dale, and were often pleasantly surprised as we found the house, or walked around to the back yard. I wanted them all to win and they already have, judging by the look of pride they wore as they showed us their gardens.

I didn't keep the contestants' names, so I can't share them with you, but I can tell you that Licking County is blessed with creative and dedicated gardeners.

We got out of the car at one house next to a perfectly trimmed bed of ivy surrounding a tree. The grass stopped, three inches of dirt all around, and ivy cut straight three inches high. "So that's what I need to do to keep the edges crisp and the ivy thick," I thought to myself. We walked around back, mouths watering at the scent of burgers on the grill. Raised beds all around, and a perfect circle of pinks in the middle, about three inches thick and ready to bloom. "How do you get your pinks like that?" I asked. (Mine spread every direction, and lean toward the light.)

She told me her secret. "I use 12-12-12 fertilizer, and I always put it on the second week of March. I have a thing about that." That will go in my calendar for next year.

At another house, a man opened the door and broke into a big grin as we explained why we were there. "That'd be my wife," he said. Soon she came out, smiling even more than he did, and began to show us her garden. He peeked out the front door, and she said, "I can't believe you did this!" He had entered her garden in the contest. He told her, but she hadn't believed him. She acted miffed, but she really wasn't.

Another couple proudly stood by as we judged their "beauty spot". They had lost a tree there, and had to have it cut down. She insisted they put a section of the trunk on the pile of dirt remaining so she could set some object on it. One thing led to another, and in a small space, we found bird feeders, art works, small paths indented in the mulch ("I take the high road and he takes the low road," she joked.) and flowers planted in the shape of the American flag, the Ohio flag, the Peace sign, and the Ying Yang symbol. I envied their creativity.

Another home owner was in the process of re-vamping his entire side yard. He had cleaned out a wooded area, built some raised beds, added stone walls as edging, and built gravel paths of white stones as accents. He explained his plans for the next two layers. He didn't need us to tell him it is going to be wonderful when it is done.

At another site, the lady of the house walked us around back. There at the rear of a large backyard was a wooden cottage with a rustic picket fence around it. The entire cottage yard burst with flowers and vines. A work boot planted with hen and chicks was nailed to a fence post, and a pair of baby shoes, also planted, echoed them at the base of the post. We spied a ring of stones hidden among the flowers. "That's for the grandkids to roast marshmallows," she said. A sleepy 3- or 4-year old came out the back door looking for his grandma. She said kids came there to play all the time. I could see why.

I loved every garden I saw that day. But we had guidelines to follow, and we did our best to keep those.

One garden sticks with me because it was done with such a love of gardening and such attention to detail that made it my favorite. This small garden devoted every available inch to plants, or artifacts, or enjoyment of those. Statues of fairies, bird feeders, ceramic frogs, wooden creations, even bowling balls, were hidden everywhere so that as you walked past a shrub or around a corner, you fund a surprise waiting. A carport became an outdoor sitting room with toys and antiques, so that I expected to see lace curtains at the non-existent windows. Years of building and collecting, growing and nurturing, had to happen to create this place.

These gardens were done by real gardeners. Thanks to all for sharing them.

FRUITS AND VEGETABLES OF YOUR LABOR

Mid-summer is a great gardening time. The spring frenzy is over - ask any garden center employee - and the plants are all settling in for the season. It's time for the gardener to relax and enjoy the fruits of his or her labor. This is a good time to take pictures of your gardens so that during planning time this winter, you can easily see what needs to be changed or added.

Soon, vegetables will be reaching their peak production. This year we tried two we had never planted before, chard and okra. The chard has beautiful colored stalks and the deer love it. We haven't gotten any yet. Okra is a pretty plant, like a little umbrella with pointy okras reaching upward between the leaves. I look forward to trying it soon.

Our asparagus was a big hit this year. It's in the fourth year, so we felt free to take considerable cuttings for a month or so. Now we are letting them all mature and build strength for next year. This bed, well-tended, should last for many years.

We have hills of cucumbers, cantaloupes, and watermelons. Our radishes, a sacrifice crop, accompanied the carrots nicely till Jim tore them out. I learned the sacrifice term from a TV program. The theory is that the bugs go for the radishes and leave the other plants alone. Bugs like the leaves. But it sure makes it sound better when you say they're a sacrifice plant. Almost like it was intentional.

A large part of our vegetable garden is devoted to onions and tomatoes. We plant onions early in the spring and enjoy so many that I begin to worry that we'll run out. So we plant them more times until a good portion of our garden is filled with gray-green spikes. A few have beautiful seed pods at the top of the stem, like a huge, white Christmas ornament. The garlic we tried this year is struggling, but we hope it produces enough to use as seed for next year's crop.

Our most productive plant is the zucchini. We harvest two or three often. A friend once told me that you didn't have to plant zucchini to get them; you just had to know somebody who planted them. Wonder if our neighbors like them?

We planted heirloom tomatoes again this year and tried a couple new varieties. We found them delicious last year. They aren't beautiful, at least most of them, but the taste is far better than the hybrid varieties. Most people, though, seem to be more concerned that they are a bright red, perfectly shaped sphere. Last year's drought hardly fazed the

Mortgage Lifters and the Pink Brandywines. My favorite was probably the rainbow, a yellow tomato with faint red streaks through the middle. We added two more this year, an heirloom cherry tomato and an Amish paste tomato.

Jim's favorite vegetable for now is the carrot patch. He pulls out three or four small carrots every evening, washes them off and shares this golden offering with me as if it were the Hope Diamond. And to us it is.

GARDENING FROM SCRATCH

If you've ever baked a "scratch" cake, you know the benefits of starting with a clean slate, choosing all new ingredients, and feeling the pride of creation. Gardening from scratch can have the same benefits.

Some friends built a house a year ago and hadn't gotten around to landscaping it yet. I volunteered to design the foundation plantings. You, too, can do this, whether you are starting with a clean slate or an overgrown landscape.

The first step was to talk with them to see what things they wanted. At first, they told me, "Whatever you like will be fine," but as we talked, I began to hear things: "red leafed maple", "What are those silver things that I see in everyone's yard?"

Knowing my friend, I knew she like things neat and orderly, so I put that into my list as well. (She probably wouldn't like an English style garden.) I also knew that they were not able to do any maintenance, so everything would have to be as care-free as possible. She mentioned the loss of a gift we had given them several years ago for their fiftieth anniversary - a flowering crabapple tree. They had left it at their last house, afraid that it wouldn't survive the move. She missed it. I told her we'd find a place in the plan for another one. She asked about fragrance several times, so I made a mental note.

I could see that some things I showed her pictures of weren't things she would like, and I scratched those from my list. We talked about a color scheme and decided on pink and white. My mind was jumping ahead to possibilities. I wanted to get to my books and a sketch pad, but there was still more work to do.

The second step was to walk around the house and note special conditions. The goal was to do the front of the house and one end for now. I knew it faced the hot afternoon sun, and that the driveway intensified the heat and reflection. All plants in the front would need to be heat and probably drought resistant. The end of the house is near woods, and so is partial shade.

She wanted the underneath or her front deck hidden from view, and I suggested lattice and plants. I suggested a curved bed around the deck and around the corner of the house, stopping just short of the gate to the back yard. Also, in looking at the soil, I realized it was the hard clay probably pulled up in of the house, not a likely place for healthy plants. So, the plan was to put topsoil on top of this, making raised beds for good drainage, and better plant survival. Mulch would be added - of course - and curves for easy mowing and attractive lines. One spot held a downspout, and rainwater tracks into the clay, still soggy from the rain a couple of days before. Those raised beds would be even more important that I thought.

The next step was to measure the bed sizes. We pulled some dowel rods out of the truck, and began to place them where we thought. Soon, a picture emerged. We hammered those into the ground, tied bright pink tape to the dowels, and brought out the spray to kill all the grass and weeds inside.

The next step was the most taxing mentally. I went home and drew a sketch of the house and driveway. I calculated how many cubic feet of soil and mulch we would need. I got out my plant books, and began to make a list of possibilities. I visited the nursery for ideas, and also to see what plants were left after the summer rush. I went through several books, one three inches thick, for ideas of plants in the color scheme and planting conditions we were working with.

I looked for plants I thought they would like. I chose lamb's ears for the silver leaves she mentioned. They are hardy in hot conditions and are perennials. They also form neat clumps that I thought she would like. I selected some plants that I already had, and then called several places for prices of the rest. Of three nurseries in the area, none had everything I wanted and all had the lowest prices on at least one thing. Each one made some valuable suggestions. I found a place near-by which provides pulverized topsoil and delivers in that area. Prices for delivery varied from $50 per load to free if I bought all the things from that nursery. I developed a price list and noted who would provide which item. Eventually I had a site plan that I was proud of. The end bed was my favorite as it contained fragrant plants which thrive in shade, and lots of white, pink, and greens. I felt certain she would enjoy this. The front side was the most difficult to design because of the conditions, but I hoped that the plants I selected would be attractive as visitors came up the drive.

In short, I enjoyed doing this not only because it was for some very special friends, but because it was creating a thing of beauty.

LATE SUMMER BARGAINS NOT ALWAYS SO

If you've been planning some major garden purchases, now is the time to take a look. Many garden centers are running specials on shrubs, trees, and other perennials. Over the years, I have purchased some great shrubs in August, and some bad ones.

Once I bought a dwarf rhododendron at the end of the season at 70% off its original price. I babied that thing for four years before I finally gave up and threw it away. It never did recover from a summer in a pot at the discount store parking lot. Since then, I've been a little more careful where and when I buy.

If you do buy a tree or shrub this time of year, be ready to give it lots of water and care through this growing season at least. Trim it back a little when you plant it, so it doesn't need quite as much moisture as it has been getting at the nursery, and then water weekly if it doesn't rain at least an inch.

September and October are great times to plant trees and shrubs because the growing demands are few, and all the plant's energy can be directed to developing roots for next year. Pick a cloudy day, and don't plant too deep.

Use the original soil, because if you give it lots of organic matter, the clay around the planting hole acts like a bathtub and holds water forever. You'll drown the plant eventually.

You can see the damage lack of water does to a plant as you are driving along the freeway. Notice the trees in the wooded areas. You will see huge numbers of trees which are slightly less green than the rest. You may even see trees that are totally brown. Trees that were damaged in a drought may never recover, even though ample rainfall has come since.

When your favorite shade tree starts to drop brown leaves on your lawn every week, look up and see if there is damage. One of ours is showing an entire branch in distress. I don't know if there is insect damage or drought, but it bears watching. Some trees that were damaged last year may not show signs of stress until next year, so don't discount this until a specialist tells you otherwise. Of course if a truck rammed into it, or you build a garage next to the trunk, it could be that, too.

GETTING BETTER AT PLANT PROPAGATION

My plant propagation has developed into a regular monthly activity, and is showing a higher percentage of success. Maybe I'm learning a few things. Each month since May, I made a little tour of the yard, clipping a few items from some favorite shrubs at a time. These I carry immediately to the potting bench in a bucket of water, trim and treat with rooting hormone, and stick them in small pots with potting soil. Under the sprinkler they go for a couple weeks when I can no longer stand the suspense and I pop them out of the pot for a quick inspection for roots. Many already show these, are potted up immediately and placed back where they came from.

I trim them at this time to encourage side shoots, and put them back under the sprinkler for another two weeks. By this time, they are usually hardy enough to go outside in a shady area.

I have discovered two kinds of shrubs that don't like to be constantly sprinkled on the leaves. They grow for a month or so, then decline. Both of these have soft fuzzy leaves that don't like constant dampness. I move them out of the sprinkler after they are obviously developing growth, and water them by hand underneath the leaves. They are thriving with this method.

Houseplants get a vacation outdoors

I hope you've been giving your houseplants a summer vacation outdoors. Mine get moved to the deck every summer for a humid atmosphere that they love. I never put them in direct sunlight for more than an hour or two per day. I take care to acclimate them slowly in the spring, moving them to total shade for a week or two, and very gradually move them to where they get more sun. I will bring them inside in early September after a thorough cleaning and inspection for insects.

Confession good for soul, bad for houseplants

I have a confession to make. Every one of my summer plants in containers has gone to its greater reward. I made myself a promise that I would water them dearly if necessary, but they still died. I think I used potting soil that had fertilizer added, then added my own.

I burnt them up.

The pots look great at the top of the stairs on either side, almost like pillars, but I suppose I should replace the brown plants. If anyone has the secret to container plants, I'd love to know it.

Still learning things from my neighbors

I've learned a couple of things from gardening friends recently. My neighbor found a source of free horse manure and piled it deeply on his vegetable garden early this spring. He said it was well rotted, but I doubted it. Rotted horse manure to a farm is not the same as to a gardener. Of course, his plants started to burn.

He said he had nothing to lose at that point, so he added some lime. The garden has recovered and is doing beautifully. Maybe I should have tried that on my containers.

Secret may help some, but won't help me

I planted some moonflower vines this spring, and gave many away to friends. My most successful one is about 4 feet tall right now, but a friend told me his wife's vine is up to the top of their archway trellis, and across the top.

I asked what her secret was. He said she just put a little Miracle Gro on it when she planted it. Now there's a secret.

The only problem is I took away my fertilizer license long ago, like I took away my husband's bleach license in the laundry room. We're both dangerous with chemicals.

CREATE YOUR OWN GARDEN ROOM

How would you like to add a gigantic room to your home for entertaining your friends and family? Or a 5 X 100 play room for the kids?

You might want to look outdoors. You can easily add usable space to your home by arranging your garden into outdoor "rooms". We inadvertently created such a place by adding a large deck near our kitchen, and then a brick patio apron to the deck. This has developed into our major entertaining area. I know - it sounds important, doesn't it? I used to read those words and think I was not the entertaining type, but every summer I get the urge to invite people over for a cookout on the gas grill. The deck holds more people than our home will comfortably, and we enjoy being outside. The roof protects us even in a light shower, and the entire evening sets a casual tone that guests seem to enjoy.

Garden rooms are the same concept, only applied to the lawn. You probably have a front yard, a back yard, and a side yard, and use them for different purposes, such as a kid's play area and a formal public area. Imagine further breaking down these areas into even more specialized "rooms". You might want, for example, a kitchen garden for herbs and vegetables, and a screened utilitarian space which includes the clothesline, trash barrels, potting bench, and tool shed. Everyone needs a parking area, and a front entry area. A beautiful path could connect these, with interesting views leading in and creating interest as you go from one to another.

Creating garden rooms is a three-step process. One, decide what areas you need or have, and where they should be. Two, separate them by some actual visual or suggestive dividing line. Three, concentrate on those "rooms" one at a time by decorating them with plant material, furniture, or objects.

Step one is not difficult, but might involve clustering things together that have been scattered about in the past. Moving a clothesline to a secluded spot near a storage shed, as an example, can help to group these functional tasks in a place where they can be easily screened from view.

Step two, dividing, is the most neglected and probably has the most impact. The side yard is a good example of an area with suggested boundaries, that is, the front and back corners of the house. You can accentuate these visual barriers with trees, gates, hedges, archways, vines, or other physical objects. Perhaps the only purpose for the area is to pass through to the back yard? Then add interesting views as you pass. An object of art at the rear of the side yard, an inviting swing, table or bench, or a striking tree at the rear will add a focal point to the view. Suddenly what was once a boring trek has become a place to enjoy. I plan to move a bench from the front yard, where it is never used, to the side yard as a focal point as you round the corner. Step two, dividing, can also involve thinking in terms of levels of the yard, if you live in a place like we do. We climbed up a steep slope to our vegetable garden for 20 years before finally building several side steps of brick. Those steps physically and visually connect the two levels, besides offering places to set container plants, and making an easier trek while loaded down with produce for the kitchen. They also make a prettier view from our back door. I originally planned to use all the steps for plants, but found it more attractive with two large matching pots at either end of the top step. This serves as a visual entry point of sorts to the vegetable garden level of the garden.

The last step, the most enjoyable part, is decorating the rooms with plant material. A large lawn can be daunting to a beginning gardener. Dividing it into rooms can make the task seem a lot less overwhelming. I try to concentrate on one area per year. Propagating plant materials you already have makes this an enjoyable, rewarding, and inexpensive process.

FALL DECORATIONS? BRING THE OUTDOORS IN

If you're like me, you love natural things. There's something about Mother Nature that is better than any man-made decoration. You can use those natural things to decorate your home for the fall, and bring in the feel and fragrance of the outdoors. Trust me, you don't have to be a genius at art, either. You might need to purchase some florist's wire or tape or other helps to create your masterpiece, though.

That said, put that fall jacket on, grab your pruning shears and a bucket or bag and head outdoors. Look for greenery of all types, dried material that is interesting, pine cones, seed heads, anything with texture, color, or fragrance. Hydrangea blooms are gorgeous by now, dried to a paper-thin beige that will last for years. Note: do NOT put them in water. Be sure to cut them with plenty of stem, and consider next year's plant as you cut. In other words, cut just above a leaf node or joint and shape the plant as you go. It's just as easy to cut a plant well as to cut it badly. If it needs thinning, cut a branch down to the base, leaving more room for the others. If it has gotten leggy, cut many branches shorter, making a shape as you go. You don't have to use all of it. Next spring you'll be pleasantly surprised with your "new" shrub.

Other treasures are pine, spruce, holly and dried seed heads from plants like rudbeckia, teasel (in the woods or along the road), coneflower, ornamental grasses — many plants qualify. Get your prettiest vases and containers out, and be creative here, too. A pitcher or galvanized container can be equally attractive done with imagination. Collect ribbons, beads and other trinkets that can create a theme. Perhaps your grandmother's antique can become the centerpiece, with your own plants around it. Take a walk around your home and look for interesting objects to add to the mix. Think tall, wide, and flat. Table centers, mantelpieces, door handles and piano tops can all benefit from some autumn cheer.

Take your treasures indoors or to the picnic table outside. Remember that pine branches seep black sticky stuff that you won't appreciate on your dining room table. Be sure to cover any surface with newspaper or plastic. Take a look at what you have, and decide how to put it together. Florist wire is thin, easily managed, and green so that it doesn't show, at least in evergreen material. Pine cones can be wired, glued, painted, glittered and fragranced within an inch of their lives. Of course, the more glitter and oil, the less nature. But it's still fun.

I have a friend that once asked us for some pine cones from our property to decorate with. I could have filled a pickup truck with them, but she demurely asked only for a small bucket full. The following year, she asked me for some more of those small pine cones. I said I didn't think we had any. She said she was sure we did. We looked, and there they were. She was appreciating what we had better than we did, simply because she had brought them inside.

You have perhaps noticed I haven't told you what to do next. That's because the best part is creating it yourself. Good luck. And don't forget to brag.

EXPERTS SHARE INFO ABOUT PLANTS

In my email this week was the Buckeye Yard and Garden letter, sponsored by the Ohio Extension Service and the Ohio Nursery and Landscape Association. Their experts get together via phone to share information about plants, diseases and insects. Several timely items follow.

As of their call, they reported that no rainfall had occurred in Columbus in September, but year-to-date totals were minus only .6 inches. Year-to-date totals can be deceiving. It's better to look at growing season totals for a real picture of what is happening. Translation: our rain this year has been clustered rather than evenly spread throughout the growing season.

I was happy to see that my own experience is validated by the experts. Though lots of plants are stressed and looking bad right now, sweet autumn clematis is looking great all over the state. According to these experts, this is a rampant clematis that can grow 10 to 20 feet in height and cover whatever structure it's growing on. Flowers are white, about an inch and a quarter across, lightly fragrant and literally cover the vine. It blooms late August into September, and sometimes as late as October. I have to duck to walk through my arbor now, and its flowers decorate the view from my kitchen window. If you're looking for a tough plant with late season bloom, consider this one.

Have any of you missed those Asian Lady Beetles yet? Any collection of water, even small amounts, can help to multiply these disease-carrying insects. Solution: take away the saucers. Note: fish ponds don't count, because the fish graciously eat the little critters before they are hatched. At least that's my theory. If you need information about repelling or preventing mosquitoes, a good amount is provided on the Ohio Department of Health and Ohio State University web sites, including alternatives to spraying programs.

To avoid being bitten by mosquitoes, refrain from using lights outside, or use yellow lights. If you plan to be out in the late evening, wear a light-colored long-sleeved shirt and long pants, and apply an effective mosquito repellent.

Orange Tennis Show Award: Two experts reported that signs of rust in lawns and calls on the topic were increasing. Susceptible varieties of Kentucky bluegrass and perennial ryegrass are turning up with the brightly colored, powdery mass that clings to fingers, clothing, shoes, and dogs' feet. According to the report, this disease will rarely kill a lawn, but it does make your tennis shoes look pretty bad.

LANDSCAPE PROFESSIONALS WORTH THE PRICE

After much thought, deliberation and frustration this summer, I finally made the decision to hire a professional to straighten out our entryway planting area.

This week, it finally happened. When I left for work, the crew was digging out years of overgrown and poorly selected plants. When I returned, they were putting the finishing touches on an area that looked so nice I almost didn't recognize it.

A tall River Birch is the focal point, surrounded by three small boulders that add contrast to the dark mulch. Lining the entire curving bed is a row of dwarf spirea still holding tiny blooms from the summer. Backing those up is a series of round dwarf evergreens. At the far end is a group of four Oakleaf Hydrangeas, a plant that I love. A small Japanese Maple graces the front door, though right now it's a little shy of leaves.

There are great swaths of dark hardwood mulch underneath, looking neat and trim. The plants are small right now, except for the River Birch (white bark calls attention to it), but over the years will fill in and add greatly to the front entryway. As I usually say when I decide to take a step like this, "Why didn't we do this years ago?"

We grow so used to seeing what we're seeing that we don't see it anymore. When the new planting is in, or the new carpet or the new paint job, we think, "How could we have accepted that for so long and not seen how jaded it had become?" I guess it's easy or we wouldn't do it so often. As is the case when we get new carpet or new paint, suddenly all the surrounding things look less attractive. In this case, we opted not to do the bed on the opposite side of the walk now, for two reasons. One was cost, but the other was the primary reason. We have a brick walk held in by landscape timbers. Over the years, it has grown mosses between the bricks, and allows small weeds to creep in. The walk meets a concrete porch. The designer had succeeded building up the slope by the walk with sandstone block. I like the idea of building up the slope, but was concerned that we were getting too many materials in a small area. As my architect nephew said, "There's something to be said for consistency."

So delaying the decision on the landscaping will allow me time to think about the walkway and research costs on replacing it with concrete. What it doesn't do is give me any relief on the nasty contrast between the two beds on either side of the walk. I guess we'll have to learn to live with that for a while. According to past experience, if I wait long enough, it won't bother me anymore!

AUTUMN TIDYING

Beautiful crisp fall days. Bright mums lining the walks. Furnaces and air conditioners idle. School busses passing by, children waving. Big red tomatoes clinging to vines. Thoughts of maple syrup and Halloween parties. Hints of the colors to come on the trees overhead. Deer checking out escape routes at the edge of the highways. Hunters parked along roads at rivers and woods, wearing camouflage and chatting about their day. Gardens scattered with pale yellow or brightly colored leaves. Spiders building webs. Morning fogs. Riding bicycles on crunchy leaves.

What could be better than autumn in Ohio? Not much, as far as I'm concerned. Florida should be jealous.

It's time to look at flower beds and vegetable gardens. Annuals that are past their prime can go to the compost pile. (You do have one, don't you?) Ditto for vegetables that have completed their task. Perennials that you don't want to leave through the winter for their structure or winter interest can be trimmed and the beds cleared of the trimmings. Some plants look great sprinkled with snow, or have seed heads that attract birds through the winter. Give yourself a treat and leave these until March so that you can enjoy nature at your windows.

Don't leave things lying on the soil that could harbor insects or disease through the winter. Put them in the compost pile for a few months, and you can return them to the soil as free fertilizer. Cleaning the beds is a great way to appreciate the fall and to feel good all winter as you look at neat beds outlined under the snow. If we get any, that is.

Once the extra plant material is gone, it's easy to see what's left. Think about how your plants did this year. Was that shrub struggling for two or three years? Many plants struggled this year in the heat and lack of rain. One that hasn't performed well over several years should be moved or discarded. Is it in too wet a spot? Too hot? Too dry? Remember that concrete, asphalt, block and brick hold heat and add to the heat of a western or southern exposure. It takes a drought-resistant plant to withstand a spot like that. The same plant in a northern or eastern location might flourish. Move it once. If it doesn't succeed in the second spot after a couple of years, it doesn't deserve to be in your yard. Get something that appreciates you.

If you move a plant, treat it like a brand-new addition, even though you're friends. Transplanting usually involves loss of roots, which means it will need extra care for a while. You might want to prune back the top to reduce moisture demands, depending on the type of plant, but never more than 1/3 of the existing top-growth per year. Water before the killing frost, mulch well, and if you're shoveling snow, add a few scoops around this plant, so that when the snow melts, it will get a special drink. Gardening in the fall is very different from springtime. Spring is harried and pressured. Fall is leisurely and non-demanding. Take advantage of this time to garden in the cool comfort of our Ohio autumn.

LIFETIME GARDENER SHARES, APPRECIATES PLANTS

There are some days that gardening looks like a mountain to climb. Lifting is harder every year, digging seems impossible, weeding interminable. Poor me.

But the alternative is worse. Looking at flower beds poking out with weeds and weak plants is the worst punishment a gardener can have. So, I plan carefully for the coolest part of the day, and I spread the work out so that the heaviest work is in small chunks of time. I think of it as exercise for the body and the soul. The irony is I usually feel better after I do the gardening than when I was sitting in the chair worrying about it.

I was heartened to hear from a reader, Ms. Ella, who wrote to say I was right about the spring rains. They sure have helped the crabgrass take over. She also tells me she has a Passion Vine that is seeding itself with lots of starts coming up in the spring.

"I've always loved to share with others," she says, reflecting the gardener's joy of sharing. Those pass-along plants get more precious every year. She's lived in her home for 62 years, and "Many flowers are running out," she says.

Some plants have a natural life span, I believe, and others need to be dug up and divided occasionally to keep going. But others will thrive for years with total neglect. Down in the strip mine country of southern Ohio, I have seen deserted homesteads, houses torn down, strip mines come and gone, with rows of daffodils still blooming after years of no attention. Now that's a plant!

Some of her plants must be thriving, however, because she says the money plants, lycoris, and hardy red lilies are blooming beautifully. She has a very old purple magnolia tree that she never trimmed.

"Years ago, we never trimmed shrubs." Fashions and practices change, even in gardening. "Most years," she says, "the shrub has a few seed pods, but this year the limbs are hanging from the weight of the pods." She goes on, "The pods are very green now, but when ripe turn beautiful red. I have planted the seed and given away the small trees, but many seeds under the trees have fallen and taken root. There are many now growing to give away."

"This has to be a female tree," she says, probably because it, too, is giving to others and producing new life.

I don't know about the sex of the tree, but I know Ms. Ella is a generous lady, as well as a lifetime gardener. She sure knows how to appreciate plants.

She is 91 this year. Atta girl, Ms. Ella!

TAKE YOUR GARDENING QUESTIONS TO LOCAL EXPERTS

The scientists at the Ohio State University Extension office regularly send me news about conditions gardeners might be interested in. For instance, Japanese beetles appeared in Ohio in mid-June to do their chewing on your plants. Soon, hordes will be visible appearing to eat everything. According to the scientists, we may be asking, "What DON'T Japanese Beetles eat?"

Magnesium deficiency is showing up on red maples (Acer Rubrum). Leaves may show yellowing between the veins and young twigs dying on the tips. Call the extension office for more information.

Tomatoes in some areas are showing what's called blossom end rot. This is a dark black spot on the bottom (opposite the stem) of the ripening tomato.

According to the extension office, it is caused by a low concentration of calcium in the soil. In my experience, it happens when not enough water has been present during the fruit's development, and if those conditions change, later fruits will not have the problem. Be patient. In Ohio, the weather will change.

These experts are a terrific resource, available to residents of this county through the Ohio Extension office. They answer questions from, "How do I know if my canner will explode beans all over the ceiling?" to "What is making those graduated holes up the trunk of my pine tree?" Answers are, "We can check the pressure." and "a yellow-bellied sapsucker." Anyway, that's what I think they said when I called years ago with these problems. They didn't even laugh. At least while I was still on the phone.

'I called them again this week. My sister-in-law found a number of dead bats in her barn. A few kept appearing every day for several days, and she was concerned. She knows I think bats are a good thing, as they eat many insects like mosquitoes that carry diseases. I offered to call the extension office to ask if they had heard of any problems in the area.

Before I got around to it, Jim found a bat in distress on our patio. When I called them, I talked with several different persons over the course of a couple of days, and most said that it's not unusual for dead bats to be found occasionally. But when they happen in groups, there is probably a reason.

The most common reason is that insecticide has been used in quantity in the area. Since a large swampy area is below my sister-in-law's house, I assumed that someone (state officials) sprayed that area for mosquitoes. The extension person said, "That's the problem with using insecticides. It affects lots of species eventually."

In more pleasant news, butterflies are beginning to grace our flowerbeds. I heard a story from one of the entymologist (bug doctors) whose neighbor mentioned how much she loved butterflies. He said, "Well, I saw you killing them two weeks ago."

She was shocked. "Me? Of course not. I love butterflies!"

"Weren't you spraying the caterpillars?"

She was silent.

We all love them when they're fluttering around the flowers. But green, wiggly and munching on our beloved plants? No way.

TREES AND SHRUBS ADD VALUE TO PROPERTY

We have a friend who doesn't want his wife to plant any trees or shrubs on their property, because he would have to mow around them. Ah yes. You can imagine what their lawn looks like - a very neat but plain expanse of grass. The opposite extreme is the lawn dotted with checkerboard plantings, each with tufts of grass sticking out at the bottom. A lawn with a bad hair day.

Trees and shrubs are part of the "bones" of a landscape plant. Their presence can add greatly to the value of your home, reduce heating and cooling costs, and improve the appearance of the house. They are called bones because they give structure to the plantings. Other plants like perennials and annuals can be added around these items for decoration and filling in. If you don't have "bones", you don't have shape and form. Or shade. Trees should frame your home, visible from behind and in front without blocking the view to your home.

"So what?" you say. So, trees and shrubs are probably on sale right now at your landscape center. These centers need to move these items so they don't have to store and maintain them all winter. If you buy them and plant them, they can be growing roots all winter so they are ready next spring to start their top growth on your property. if you want to get a bargain price and enjoy the best planting time all year, this is it. Late fall.

As you pick a tree, consider shade, color, shape, height, root habit, fruit, and wind protection. For the south and west side of your house, you might want a shade tree. These cool your house in summer, reducing cooling costs, and drop their leaves in the winter to let the sunshine in and warm your house for free. When the leaves are out, they graciously use up carbon dioxide and put out oxygen to freshen your air. They catch dust and particles on their leaves, waiting for the rain to rinse it gently to the ground, and clean your air constantly. Some varieties live hundreds of years. What better friends can there be in the plant world? Recently I met a tree whose arm (branch) was bent to point to the nearby river. It was almost 150 years old, still pointing to the river.

If you choose a shade tree, make sure you get one whose roots don't tend to stick out of the soil as it grows. This makes for bumpy lawnmower rides, and dulling of the blades. Ask me how I know this. Some of the best shade trees are the ones you see everywhere: maples and oaks. If you want wind protection in the wintertime, plant these on the side of your home the prevailing winds come from. Since most wind protection is needed in the winter, you will need evergreens for this. Remember that these can get quite wide at maturity, so don't plant them right against your house. You'll be sorry years later. Maybe the side yard?

If you hanker for a fruit tree (or orchard) of your own, these can be a conversation piece in your backyard. I have an apple and a cherry tree, and may get another this year. There's nothing more fun than picking fresh fruit on your own property year after year. If you plan to do this, you need to be willing to spray at appropriate times of the year to get the best production and quality fruit. There are three sizes of many fruit trees: standard, semi-dwarf, and dwarf. If you want ease of picking, the dwarf sizes are for you. They also bear years earlier than the standard sizes.

The staff of the nursery or landscape center has lots of knowledge about growth habits and needs of each tree type they sell. Take advantage of their skills and ask them for advice. They're paid for their knowledge and to help you.

Recently my husband was digging through old pictures, and found an early one of our home. He was amazed at the size and lack of trees thirty years ago. It seems like yesterday I made a decision to plant at least one new tree per year on our property. Now our first Christmas tree is forty feet high in full view of the front window, and many others create shade and atmosphere,.

Trees make a home inviting if chosen and placed well. Planting a tree is an investment in the future.

CONSIDER SIMPLICITY AND COLOR

My husband and I just returned from a trip through central Kentucky. I didn't realize how beautiful Kentucky is.

We passed through the horse country in Lexington, where huge homes and horse farms boast miles of grassy pastures, white fences and driveways with names like Blue Ribbon Drive. After a while, I noticed the simple understating of the plantings. Most were huge trees and simple spots of single colors, often at the driveway entrance. The effect was magnificent and peaceful. I saw many ferns in hanging pots or pedestals at the front door. This planting style may be a result of climate, long-established homes, or other interests like horses. But, since I saw the same influences in smaller, suburban homes, I eventually decided that it was a cultural tradition in the area.

That led me to wonder what our cultural traditions are in this area. Sometimes it's easier to see others' traditions than your own. Maybe the well-dressed concrete goose?

The trip also included a list to the Shakertown National Park in Kentucky. There, I was inspired by simplicity, which the Shakers elevated to a religion. They believed that everything should have a purpose, and that their work was a form of praising God. These beliefs were apparent in their landscaping. There were simple straight walks and fence-lined areas for movement, livestock, and gardens. Matching expanses of shade trees, vegetable gardens and herbs all were functional, as well as beautiful. At the parking lot near the entrance, a reflective pond graced by several swans met us, and calmed us from our travels. By the time we finished our tour, I was ready to simplify my own life, in my gardening and my home.

Perennials are one way to simplify your life in gardening. These beauties come back year after year and ask for nothing from you except a good spot, enough water, and maybe dividing every few years.

A recent email asked, "I'm under the impression that there aren't very many perennials for fall color. Am I wrong?" Guess what the answer is. YES! There wouldn't be gardeners if there weren't a yes answer to that and other similar questions. I looked around my own yard and found some things in bloom right now. One is my Annabelle hydrangea, a big-leaf type with huge balls of blooms. Right now it's in its second blooming period this summer. The blooms are light green, but they will eventually turn white and then tan as they dry on the shrub. I will have those to look at all winter long, and they are beautiful against the snow, when little else is visible. I often cut several blooms, put them in an empty vase and allow them to dry over the winter. Dry, they stay beautiful many years. I'm not exaggerating.

My Stella D'Oros are still blooming occasionally, and they can reliably be counted upon to bloom from mid-summer to fall. My gold flame spirea are still blooming pink with pale green foliage. I was sure I wasn't going to like this combination at first, but it is growing on me. Is that a pun? I see this plant everywhere in commercial plantings, which usually means it has lots of good traits. It is durable, reliable, and adds color in tough places, like next to concrete and asphalt, where heat is a problem.

But my favorite right now is the silver lace clematis vine, now about four years old. I started these from cuttings my sister-in-law got for me, and they are finally sizable enough to be absolutely stunning. I have two, planted at either side of a small arched arbor next to my patio. Only one is in bloom right now, and it is covered with small white star-shaped flowers. I look out the window over my sink and am treated to this lacy vine. It climbs on a wrought-iron arbor that the Licking County Vocational students made and sold.

Another shrub in bloom right now is my Late Panicle Hydrangea (h. tardiva). It, too, is covered with white cone-shaped blooms and has been for two or three weeks. My Oakleaf hydrangea should be coming into its own next season, with leaves that turn red in the fall. This is a four-season plant, with winter interest from the panicles and rough bark, spring foliage of long green oak-like leaves and summer bloom.

Don't forget that green is a color, too, and nothing is more peaceful than a shady nook filled with varieties and shades of green colors.

Color can be achieved by flowers, foliage or fruit. All of these are interesting to watch as they change, can bring birds or wildlife to your property and add greatly to your property value and quality of life.

WHEN IN DOUBT, ASK A
FRIEND FROM THE HILLS

On a trip to West Virginia last week, we visited a friend whose home is in a national forest. His lawn is literally carved out of the woods.

Loosely around the inner edge of the lawn were a number of mid-sized evergreens, tightly trimmed to a perfect cone shape. Instantly, my mind jumped to Alice in wonderland and the queen for some reason. Even the leader, or the main trunk, appeared to have been cut. They were beautifully green and healthy in spite of their artificial shape. Or maybe because of it?

I asked, "Who trims the evergreens?"

She answered, "Oh, Bill does. He finally got smart and uses the machete."

Later, Bill elaborated. "At one time, we had 1,500 pine trees, and I used to trim them all with hedge trimmers." He made a motion with his elbows out and hands moving toward the center of his chest. I got tired thinking about it.

"I guess you didn't have to use the bicep machine at the YMCA," I said weakly.

"Nope. Then when they got big, I had to do it from a ladder. Eventually, I figured out the machete was much faster and easier. Zip, zip and I'm done."

I told him my evergreens were a little straggly in places, and I had pruned them lightly for a couple of years so they were gradually thickening up. "Oh, you have to prune them," he said. He reminded me of the vineyard manager who told me the same thing about my grapes with a somewhat disapproving scowl.

The shrubs proved his point. All were solid, thick, and green. I think the machete method is a little harsh, and doesn't allow for a natural look, but I wasn't about to argue with a machete-bearing hillbilly. (Since I'm married to one, I can call them that.)

The point is PRUNE. Prune out that extra leader - no tree, club or country needs two leaders. Prune out dead areas. Prune the tips out of sparse branches to encourage side growth and thickening up. Prune the length of the branches and promote symmetry. You can even shape it into Mickey Mouse if you want. Then it's called a topiary.

Timing is critical for conifers, because they are likely to bleed when cut. Autumn and winter are good times to prune them, as it keeps bleeding to a minimum. So anytime during the resting seasons of fall and winter is fine.

Another method with conifers is to "candle" them. That means taking the tip out of the branches (or the candle - the new growth) by simply pulling on the tuft of needles at the end of the branch that you want to fill out more, or out of all the branches. Try it. It works, and it doesn't cause bleeding by the gardener. If you want to test the theory, take a picture before you do this. Then take a picture next year during mid-season. See if you can see the difference in the growth pattern and shape. You'll be hooked. I guarantee it.

THE TIMES THEY ARE A'CHANGING

Can you smell it? Can you feel it? Fall is in the air. Oh, we'll probably have more hot days, but everyone knows it's coming. This week I saw a tree with one branch turned bright orange. The birds are disappearing, the frogs are heading for better territory, and the possums aren't crossing the rural roads defying the cars that speed by.

The backpacks are filled, the kids are in school, and life goes on. Even the slowing down is part of the cycle. The plants have worked hard all summer, and now are winding their season down. Our bodies know it, too. Instinctively, we change our behavior. We start to think more chili and fewer salads — unless we fight that urge. Recently, I heard a lady say she was ready for corduroys and sweaters.

I don't know if I would go that far, but I love the change of seasons. Each one brings new promises, new temperatures, new things to do and see and appreciate. Gathering in is the hallmark of this season. How can you resist those beautiful leaves, those bright red tomatoes, those sparkly mums at every front door?

Plan a trip with your family to a pumpkin farm this fall, and make it a tradition that the whole family enjoys. Gather mums and decorate for Halloween or Fall Harvest. Enjoy the crisp clear fall days. Take a walk through a nearby park, and inhale the crisp air. Cruise the bike trails and say hello to your neighbors. Walk the paths of state, county, or city parks nearby. Sit on the hills and think about Indians as they may have enjoyed the same space.

You don't have to be a gardener to enjoy the seasons, but it helps. Getting your hands dirty in the soil, and your nose next to the plants makes you notice things. Fall means we have less rain, and the plants react to that by gently slowing down their growth. Sunlight is shorter, and temperatures ease. If we take time to look, we can see the stars at night and white puffy clouds in the day, thanks to lower humidity.

I won't notice this as I can tomatoes probably, but it will be there.

My Autumn Joy Sedum is about to burst into its full glory, and the bees are noticing. They are busily gathering for the winter.

Apparently the terrorists are busy too. I am looking at pictures on television. It feels like Beirut. I wonder what can be next, the same feeling I had after Oklahoma City and JFK's assassination. We got through those, and we'll get through this, hopefully stronger.

GREENHOUSE GIVES PLANTS A HEAD START

One of my children did an experiment for school during the late '70's.

That same year, we had decided to try a small greenhouse for plants in pots and houseplants. My husband built a lean-to frame with two-by-fours and covered it with plastic, sloped on the front with a door, and totally open at the back. We shoved it up on the patio on the cement to the pair of windows in our kitchen. We opened the windows to allow some heat to enter the greenhouse. Obviously, the unit was not sealed at any point and leaked air all around where it met the house.

The windows allowed heated air from the house to keep the greenhouse warm during the night, and heated solar air to enter the house during the day. We did not attach it to the house or seal the edge. We merely pushed it up against the house. For a school assignment, my son began to keep records and take pictures.

Remember the year of the blizzard? That was the year. On the day the blizzard struck, it was 25 below zero at noon outside. Inside the greenhouse, it was 70 degrees! This is the solar energy that a greenhouse collects. Even a leaky aired one! I think the concrete floor was the key.

Before the blizzard struck, we learned the magic of a greenhouse for plants. We started new houseplants almost without effort, deep green and sturdy. The humidity and bright light are magic ingredients that no house can provide.

A year ago, I began to learn how to grow things in a real greenhouse. We found some plans that called for inexpensive, easily assembled materials for a freestanding one, and took the plunge. Our plans were from North Carolina Cooperative Extension Service, are available on the internet, and were designed for home use.

As I called around the area to get bids on electric and plumbing, I often got comments like, "Oh, I'd love to have a greenhouse!" I realize that for some, the novelty can wear off, and the greenhouse fall into disrepair and neglect. If this is your pattern, don't bother with a greenhouse. Get a cold frame or a potting bench. You can do a great deal with these, and they are much less obtrusive.

My interest hasn't waned yet. My greenhouse is my favorite place to be, especially in the spring and fall when gardening is limited outside. It is possible to grow fruits and vegetables out of season in the greenhouse. Cold weather plants such as lettuce and cabbage can grow all winter. So can warm weather plants such as tomatoes, if you're willing to keep it warm enough.

What do I use it for? I have started many bedding plants for the summer, wintered over geraniums from cuttings, started a hundred shrubs, many ground covers, and created many gifts there. I found a pea and grew one pea plant there this winter. My husband ate every pea pod that grew....

I try to keep plants started to give to visitors and I have had to increase the number of those over time. I have given houseplants a vacation there, and fought off an insect invasion for the first time.

I tried a variety of herbs, flowers, shrubs and hanging pots, and learned which can take the cool winter temperatures.

If you're a gardener, the thrill of stomping snow off your boots as you enter a warm, humid, bright garden smelling of damp earth and blooming geraniums simply cannot be described. Maybe I just did.

The best part is the ability to have a wider selection of plants than you can get at a nursery, and to increase the number of plants that you have. I tell my husband that I don't spend less at the nursery, I just spend it on different things.

Besides, it's cheaper than medicine or therapy. I take my radio, my phone, and my dog, and I don't have to come in for hours. I have plants growing in my yard now that I started on New Year's Day. Next year, maybe I'll have a millennium garden.

BUDDING AND GRAFTING
FOR ADDING TREES

I made an error in judgment today. I went berry-picking with my husband and my sister-in-law. They've been picking berries for more years than they would like me to share, and they love it. Now I like to grow berries, but picking is not my favorite thing. So when I got tired, I wandered back to the sales room at Highwater Orchard to weigh my blueberries and choose some other fruit (already picked, of course). I assumed they would follow me back shortly.

Since it was a hot day, and the store was air-conditioned, I looked for an excuse not to go back outside. I asked the owner if they started their own trees. She said yes, they had started most of them as "whips," or one single stem that eventually filled out into a tree.

"Did you ever start them from cuttings?" I asked. "No but we occasionally graft trees to scion stock, and have also budded some." She wrinkled her nose slightly when she mentioned budding, which piqued my interest.

I nodded to show my vast understanding of the term "scion". I remembered vaguely reading about that term for the root stock of a grafted tree.

"What's the difference between budding and grafting?" I asked. She said grafting is actually cutting off a young tree and sort of slipping another tree stalk into the first. Then you seal and wrap the joint until it grows together and you get a new tree.

With budding, you just insert a tiny leaf bud (leaf joint or node) from one tree into another. "It's very tedious," she said. Once the bud "takes", the original trunk is removed, and the bud is allowed to become the new tree.

You're probably wondering why you would cut up a perfectly good tree to insert another. There are a lot of reasons, but for fruit trees, it can be to produce a dwarf or semi-dwarf tree, which is easier to pick from than a full-sized one.

"I've been wanting to try grafting since I saw a TV program about a man who created multi-colored evergreen topiaries by grafting different varieties together. It looked like fun." She smiled patiently. I asked, "Why don't you like budding?"

"You have to do it in August, and it's HOT in August." Don't I know it. "But you do grafting in March, and that's a slow time for us."

I was beginning to understand. "Plus it's cool in March," I said. Now it was my turn to smile. This was a woman after my own heart.

I glanced out of the window and saw two hot and sweaty bodies struggling up the hill with heavy buckets. "He's going to brag about how many more berries he picked than me," I said. "Let's weigh these before he gets here." One and a half pounds - a respectable effort.

When they came in, Bonnie explained that they had been racing to fill their buckets. Hers weighed in at four pounds. Jim pushed his berries toward the cash register. "Five pounds," she announced after weighing his.

"How much did hers weigh?" he immediately asked, nodding in my direction. I was hoping she'd lie, but she didn't.

MULCH, MULCH!

One of the secrets to low maintenance gardening is mulch. You knew I was going to say it, didn't you? Mulch conserves moisture, discourages weeds, protects the soil from pounding or washing away during heavy rains, improves all types of soils, and even improves the appearance of your plants. In gardening, it's a panacea. Get some!

A critical part of low maintenance gardening is plant selection. Don't choose plants that need pampering, are drought-sensitive, or are susceptible to diseases and insects. How do you know? Ask your nursery plant person. (The guy at the grocery or discount store won't have a clue.)

Perennials, those plants that come back year after year, meet some of these criteria by definition of perennial. With little attention, they reappear and even multiply. Obviously, they don't need to be purchased and planted every year as annuals do. Deadheading, which is removing spent flowers, isn't necessary, but may improve flowering and appearance. You may need to divide some types every few years or stake the taller ones, but that is small price to pay for their beauty and reliability.

A word of caution: No plant will grow in a place unsuited for it. It it's not happy, move it or even pampering won't save it. If you plant a drought-sensitive plant in the hot afternoon sun, you'll spend a lot of time watering, and the plant may still struggle. So if it prefers shade, move it there quickly and treat it gently for a while till it recovers. Besides, moving things around is part of the fun. When you find the right spot, both you and the plant will know it.

I just noticed that I tend to talk about plants as if they are people, which to me they are. If you spend time with them, you get to know their personalities and habits. Then it's obvious when they're not happy. They show it, just like a person you know very well.

A perfect low maintenance garden usually doesn't require watering, but whose garden is perfect? In drought and extreme heat such as we sometimes have, watering can save some plants that might otherwise be lost from stress. Even if the perennials lose some of their beauty this year, next year they'll be back as beautiful as ever, provided we don't neglect them into oblivion.

A low maintenance garden wouldn't have a hedge that needs trimming a couple of times a season, or shrubs that quickly get out of bounds and must be pruned back, or ivy that needs cut to keep it out from under the siding.

If this is happening in your garden, probably the plants are in a spot where they shouldn't be. A happy plant is where it can grow to its natural size and shape and look beautiful. If you have to constantly alter it, that's not low maintenance, nor good for the plant.

Next time you drive by a long-abandoned house, don't. Stop and take a look at the plants that survived. Trees, irises, old-fashioned roses, daffodils. Those are plants that survived with total neglect. There are many others that ask for very little, and give years of enjoyment in return.

KEEP WATERING DURING DRY SPELL

My garden is struggling. I hope that by the time you read this, we've received a drenching rain, and the grass is so high that everyone in the neighborhood is mowing his/her lawn at the same time. Noisy, but satisfying.

My son once worked for a local golf course as a greenskeeper. He took great pride in, as he put it, "doing things that golfers would like." He loved to play golf.

One summer when he worked there, it was 100 degrees many days. One day he called home to say that he and his friend Robert were the only ones playing on the golf course that afternoon. "Imagine that," I mumbled, thinking this must be his father's genes talking.

One of his jobs there was to water the greens. He spent many hours lugging equipment around the entire course, setting up sprinklers to keep the greens as healthy as possible. He told me, "Mom, just a little rain is so much better than hours of sprinkling."

I can attest to that. I wonder where all that water goes? I've been using sprinkling systems and hoses much more than I used to, and I really can't see much improvement in the plants. I guess if they're still living, that's an improvement

One thing I've never done is water our lawn. I figure if it gets brown, so be it. It'll come back later. Landscape plants are another matter. Established plants are not usually threatened by the heat, unless it is severe and prolonged. However, new plants are extremely threatened and need to be closely cared for if you like them at all and hope they'll be back next year.

Young trees especially need extra water the entire first year while they are developing an extensive root system.

Don't expect to see a lot of growth on any new plant, because underneath is where the action is the first year.

An old saying about perennials is this: The first year, they sleep; the second year, they creep; the third year, they leap! This means that they take their sweet time to do much growing, at least where it can be seen by the gardener and his or her neighbors. They plan their operation by developing their support systems, logistics and line of attack before they put on the public show. (A lesson that soldiers and community leaders would do well to emulate.)

But I digress. I try to conserve water, even though we have our own well, so I don't water needlessly. I do water to protect stressed plants, new plants, and the vegetable garden. That mulch we put on two months ago is helping tremendously to conserve any remaining moisture in the soil where we need it, but it can't do it alone.

Once when we were in a severe drought, I started collecting rinse water from my clothes washer into a plastic trash container with wheels. I figured the rinse water would have the least soap and other chemicals in it to harm the plants. I would move the hose over to the container after the wash cycle was finished. Then we would roll this out to the plants and gently dip the water onto the plants. I don't know how much this helped the plants, but it made me feel a lot better.

For now, we are using a mixture of sprinkling hoses, soaker hoses, and sprinklers, along with an assortment of faucet splitters and spray nozzles. He anyone out there ever figured out how to set one of those jiggly things that you stick in the ground? I usually back away and let Jim have a go at it.

I try to water each area every two or three days for a half hour or so in this heat, and a different area every day. This is not enough to keep the plants going strong, but I don't expect it to be. I only expect to keep them alive until the weather breaks.

We used to collect rain in a barrel at the downspout, and allow it to leak out through a soaker hose up close to the house where rain seldom reaches. I gave this up when I realized that algae and who knows what grew in that tube and eventually went on my plants. I didn't think this was healthy, especially for new plantings.

SEEDS OF FUTURE GARDENS

While traveling last week, I heard a priest tell a story about Benjamin Franklin, who received a broom from India as a gift. Franklin, an avid gardener, noticed two seeds sewn in the stitching at the top.

He gently worked them out and planted them. That was the beginning of the corn broom industry in America.

Seeds are one of God's miracles. In them is contained the entire genetic information to create a new plant. In special cases, seeds have been preserved for thousands of years, still viable.

From a seed a giant oak can grow, which our assistant gardener, the gray squirrel, regularly proves. I usually manage to dig up his efforts and put them in pots for growing on.

Seeds don't take much space, are easy to store, and are a mystery about to happen. You can ship them across country to your grandchildren.

Last year, I saved some beautiful black shiny seeds I found on my Stella D'Oro daylilies. I planted them this spring in the greenhouse, and they germinated beautifully. Some had white leaves, and those I discarded. I probably should have waited to see if I had made a great discovery, but I doubt it.

The plants have matured, but so far, no blooms. I will keep them one more year, and if they still don't have blooms, into the compost pile they'll go.

Why didn't I get Stella D 'Oro? Probably because the original flowers were hybrids, or the result of crossing two different plants or varieties for certain desirable characteristics. The seeds produced were random crossings with some other plant, or reversions to the original, with the undesirable characteristics dominant. In other words, it was a waste of time and garden space.

Did I have any successes? Yes - with the hollyhocks. At the base of the bloom is a round flattish pod where I found hundreds of flat round seeds packed together in a doughnut arrangement like records in an old-fashioned jukebox. These now grace my yard and several friends' yards, just as beautiful as the original.

My heirloom tomatoes contain my future tomatoes. Heirloom tomatoes are not hybrids, so the seeds produce plants like their parents, not rogues with unexpected flaws. I plan to create a new tradition in my family by saving tomato seeds for my children this year.

So far we have sampled Radiator Charlie's Mortgage Lifter and Pink Brandywine. The drought has drastically slowed production, but what's there is delicious. The colors are different from what we are used to and so is the taste.

How do you store seeds? It is very important to be sure the seeds and pods are completely dry before storing for the winter. Otherwise, molds destroy the seeds.

After drying them thoroughly and sorting out other material, place them in an airtight container, label carefully with color, variety, planting directions, and date collected. (Get this information from books if you don't know it already.)

You can use plastic bags that zip shut, and put them in an index box by planting date. File them according to the weeks they should be planted. For example, using the average frost-free date as the key (May 15 in this area), file them under eight weeks before, six weeks before, etc. This will keep you on schedule, but only if you remember to look in the box.

Don't forget to note whether the plants can be transplanted and thus started early indoors, or should be planted outside directly in their permanent location. Some plants resent being moved, like beets. Ask me how I know this.

The best part of seed saving is learning about plants and their habits. My eyes no longer skim over the spent flowers or vegetables in a garden. They are drawn to those pods to see if the seeds have exploded or been carried through the air, or still reside where I can capture them. I have a jar on my kitchen windowsill with two huge avocado seeds.

Don't you think an avocado tree would look nice in my greenhouse?

A FINAL CHECKLIST

You've planted your spring-blooming bulbs. You've raked and mulched your leaves, or will soon. You've harvested all your vegetables and composted the unusable ones. Your compost pile is bulging at the seams. (Don't worry, it will go down quickly.) You've cut the grass the last time of the season and everything looks neat.

Well not everything. Have you looked at your garden and flower beds? There are lots of brown skeletons there. Some are good structural interest through the winter, such as Miscanthus. This tall grass eventually turns golden and its seed heads nod gracefully through the snow storms until late February. Others are not so attractive. My mums are already spent and falling over. Iris leaves are brown on the ends and splotchy throughout. Hostas are wilting fast, except the seed heads that will stick out awkwardly all winter if you let them.

One of the last chores of the season, as you've probably guessed, is to clean up the garden. This is a satisfying job that not only improves the look of the lawn for the next six months, but also reduces the chance of diseases and insects wintering over. It provides lots of brown and green matter for the compost pile and allows the soil a chance to rest a little sooner than it would otherwise.

Will things decompose without your help? Of course. Mother Nature has been doing this for centuries. But some will persist through the first burst of growth in the spring, and will poke straggly ends through those pristine blankets of snow all winter. Trust me - it looks better without them.

Cleanup includes picking up dropped vegetables in the garden, and removing all annual plant matter in flower beds and garden, including the roots, unless it is beans or peas. These carry nodules that naturally fertilize your soil, so cut these plants off at soil level and leave the roots intact. You can trim to the ground any annuals or non-evergreen perennials still left standing.

You can cover the goldfish pond with netting to keep out the falling and blowing leaves. I've learned to leave the pond cleanup till spring, because it leaves soft material at the bottom for the snails and frogs to winter over. Too much, however, can sap the oxygen out of the water and harm the fish.

Don't cut back any evergreen plants. Pachysandra and myrtle, for example, add texture year-round. Even if your evergreen shrubs and trees need trimming, save this task for later. Last year I made two huge Christmas wreaths from boxwood and pine trimmings after Thanksgiving.

As you trim, you might want to cut some attractive plants to similar lengths, bundle them with a rubber band or string, and hang them upside down inside your house. As they dry, you can enjoy their fragrance, color and texture. In a couple of weeks they will be ready to use in arrangements or potpourri. Jim has garlic drying on the deck, and jalapeño peppers in the kitchen.

After you've finished trimming and composting, take a look around. If things are extremely bare and uninteresting, that's probably a sign you need more "bones" in your garden:

more evergreens, trees, or permanent structures such as walls, benches, or statuary. During the winter, these are all you have to contemplate.

Remember a few weeks ago when I told you I'd let you know when to stop gardening? This is it. Both you and your garden can rest for awhile. But don't be surprised if I think of something else that needs doing.

FREE FERTILIZER?

You may have seen something very valuable floating by your window lately - leaves. These are free fertilizer for your plants, if you're willing to get a little exercise. Sure, left on your lawn in a glob they'll mat down and smother the grass. But treated right and put in the right place, your soil will be much improved by them. Of course, you can hope for a big wind to carry them over to your neighbor's lawn, but why let them get away?

If you grew up associating the smell of burning leaves with fall, you'll be pleased to know that is an idea whose time has GONE, thank heaven. It pollutes the air and is a waste of a good resource.

Those leaves, chopped into small pieces, make wonderful loose, attractive mulch. My vegetable garden has benefitted for years from this soft covering. Technically, this is sheet composting, or spreading the material over a large area to decompose there, rather than in a pile. I just think of it as free mulch or fertilizer. Earthworms like to have meetings under there, and add their own blessing to my garden soil.

After a couple of years of this, the soil becomes soft and easily managed.

In October, we cover the garden a foot deep with this chopped stuff, and by March, it's only about two inches deep, perfect for planting those cold weather crops. We just pull back the mulch and stick the seeds or plants in.

Yes, leaves need to be shredded. Those that aren't shredded tend to mat down and don't get enough oxygen to decompose readily. And no, they don't blow around if they're shredded.

So how does this work? Personally, I like the old-fashioned system. Raking leaves is a great workout, with the added benefit of that cool, crisp air and a beautiful fall day. I remember my kids when they were small diving into our piles of leaves. We gladly re-piled them just to watch the glee. There are easier ways, however.

Usually I run the mower around the opposite direction from what I normally do for mowing. That is, I move the leaves to the center in a pile. After I get very close in, the leaves start blowing over the pile to the other side, so I finish with the rake.

We have metal and bamboo rakes. The bamboo rake is very wide and very light, so it's easy to cover a lot of territory. I usually get stuck with the metal one and some friendly ribbing about how slow I am.

Soon we have a huge pile of leaves in the center of our front yard. The next step is to jump in the middle and throw some leaves around. OK, that's out of your system? Now rake the pile together again and go get the leaf shredder or lawn mower.

Some leaf shredders include vacuums. Ours has a little ramp where we rake the leaves up and into the machine. It's noisy - I wear my radio headset.

We use a mesh bag to collect the shredded leaves. It's always amazing to me how a huge pile of leaves is compressed into a small bag after they're shredded.

This finished product gets carried to the garden and dumped around. Many bags later, we (usually Jim does this because I'm too tired) level it off on the raised beds and go watch football.

You don't have a shredder? Just run your lawn mower over the leaves a few times until coarsely chopped. Carry them to the garden or flower bed.

We have a lot of trees and a big yard, so leaves are plentiful. But, if you find as we sometimes do, that you need more leaves than you have, don't be afraid to ask your neighbors. They'll think you're crazy, but that's part of the fun.

DON'T STOP GARDENING JUST YET

Sorry guys, but gardening isn't over yet. September is a perfect time to do fall chores outdoors. Besides, it's beautiful outside.

Plant spring flowering bulbs now. Daffodils, tulips, irises, and crocuses are standard. You can also plant perennials. They may be on sale, so you get a lot of benefits for gardening in the fall. The plants benefit too, because every time the temperature is just above freezing, they grow roots before they have to produce that spring burst of growth.

Fall is when gardeners plan their colorful spring. I remember the first time I planted some bright red tulips. I spent a week that spring sitting backwards on my couch so I could look at them.

Most daffodils will come up for many years and grow thicker each year. I can't think of anything more cheerful than a crop of bright yellow daffodils when nothing else has poked its leaves out yet, unless it's tiny croci (crocuses) blooming in the snow. Plant daffodils in a sunny place where you won't mow off the leaves after they've bloomed and where they can freely multiply. The leaves provide energy to the bulbs for next year after the blooming is over.

You can buy tulips with early to late blooming varieties with short, mid-length, and tall stems. I like them all. Since their bloom doesn't last very long, select different blooming times so you can enjoy them longer. I recently learned that some tulips are designed to grow only one season, so they should be treated as annuals. The nursery staff should know if they are the annual type. I just assume I need to replant them every year or two. Actually I'm happy if they make it one season before they become mole food.

Be sure to plant bulbs as deep as the instructions say. I know digging a deep hole is not easy. But the tulips will last longer and look better if you do. You might try using a dibber or a bulb planter to plant them. A dibber has a T-shaped handle and a pointed end about 12 inches long. You shove this into the ground, tip it over to open the hole, drop in a bulb, and then close up the hole. With practice, you can plant a lot of bulbs in an hour. A bulb planter is a handle with a round cutter that cuts a round core out of the earth where you then drop the bulb and cover with soil.

There are many types of bulbs and your garden center can advise you on placement. My advice is to buy twice as many as you think you need and plant them in a large mass for effect.

Another fall job between now and when the ground freezes is transplanting or dividing perennials. Plants that got leggy this year or leaned out away from the house are probably in need of more sun. Move them now and don't forget to give them a few drinks of water the next couple of months. Those daffodils that aren't blooming as well as they did a few years ago would do much better if you dig them up and spread them out.

Hostas, irises and other perennials should be split in half or quartered with a shovel and replanted where they have room to stretch out. Give them a sprinkle of bone meal or slow-release fertilizer and a drink of water when they get to their new home - it's only hospitable.

Take a walk around and look for which plants are struggling where they are. Just remember that many plants may be struggling this year because of conditions. If so, don't be afraid to move them, but give them some extra care for a while until they get re-established.

If you have geraniums you like, take some cuttings to winter over. Pick some medium-sized branches, and cut off the tips about 6 inches from the end. Remove the lower leaves, leaving the top two or three inches. Insert the stem into some rooting hormone, then into a small pot of soilless mix or potting soil. Water well.

Put a wire or two sticks (pencils work) in the pot and a clear plastic bag loosely over them. Keep it open at the bottom so air can circulate. The supports are to keep the bag off the plant. Set the pot out of the sun in a warm, humid spot. Keep it damp, but not soggy. In a couple of weeks if it appears to be growing, remove the bag and put the plant in a sunny window. Transfer into a larger pot when the plant gets top- heavy, and by next spring you'll have geraniums worthy of your front steps.

As your vegetable garden wanes, clean out the spent plants to put in your compost piles. If you have beans or peas, leave the roots in the soil and remove only the above-ground parts. These plants develop nitrogen nodules on their roots - free fertilizer for your garden. Put all plant wastes not diseased or insect-infested into your compost pile. You can put green tomatoes indoors in brown paper bags in a cool dark place to ripen.

I'll let you know when you can stop gardening, but don't hold your breath.

BENCHES FOR STORAGE AND WORK

A great project this fall that is good for gardeners of any experience level is a potting bench. Why do you need one, you say?

A potting bench is probably one of the first steps toward gardening with a passion. It can be used by gardeners who love houseplants, container plants, vegetables, or those who like to propagate plants. In other words, any gardener at all. A potting bench makes a great Christmas present for your favorite gardener, with plenty of time before spring to gather supplies.

First, a bench gives you a place to store things. Before I got mine, I had planting items scattered all over the house. Now I know where everything is, and I don't have to clean up a mess when I'm done. I let the wind and rain do that.

When my patient husband built a potting beach out of scrap lumber for me, I placed it under some pines where it would be out of the sun and somewhat hidden.

I use some large vinyl tubs for holding soil mix or other ingredients. I mix my own, with various amounts of potting soil, peat moss, vermiculite, and slow-release fertilizer as planting mediums. I've learned a lot about what plants don't like. I'm still not happy with the results, but I can now vary it for specific uses.

New cuttings, for example, can be placed in vermiculite alone. Vermiculite is a white crumbly substance that holds moisture, easily penetrated by roots. It drains well, so you don't have to worry about over-watering. When the cutting is ready to be potted up, you gently lift the plant by its leaves out of the tray or pot. It comes out easily, roots wrapped around a small ball of vermiculite, and can be planted directly into regular potting soil for growing on, without disturbing the roots.

I perform all these operations at my potting bench. For example, I bring fresh cuttings in a bucket of water or plastic bag to the bench, trim them of extra leaves, or cut two large leaves in half, and put them in a tray of vermiculite. I usually trim smaller leaves to a pair of leaves at the top, with a stem at the bottom, minus the two leaves that were there. Dipping them into rooting powder at that trimmed node makes the spot where roots will grow. When I see evidence that they have rooted in vermiculite, as in growth, I can plant them into potting soil. Under the spray or into the greenhouse they go for a few weeks until my watchful eye sees a healthy plant beginning to emerge. I can then put them in a semi-sunny window and watch what happens.

Back to the potting bench for a small pot and regular potting soil, and then it is returned to the place it just left to gently adjust. After a week or two, I move it to a dryer spot more like its eventual permanent location, which may be indoors or outdoors.

Both places are harsher environments than where the plant has been, so I try to adjust it gradually.

Whenever a plant becomes too large for its pot, back to the bench we go for a larger one. The old pot is rinsed off in a tub of water with a little bleach for sterilizing, and neatly stacked by size under the bench. I no longer put off this chore because I enjoy standing in the pine needles doing what I love.

VISITORS TO GARDEN NOT ALL DEERLY LOVED

My husband's voice rang down the hill: "Jo Ann! Something pulled out the strawberry plants!" His voice showed his shock that someone would pull the plants out to lie on top of the ground, root ball and all. Who would do such a dastardly deed?

He searched further, and found carrots and beets also tossed about. The soft dry mulched ground yielded them up to any tug without a struggle.

Soon, my detective husband found a major clue - a pair of indentations in the soil. "Oh. It's a deer." He sounded disappointed. I said, "They're probably hungry,", and he didn't complain any more. Verbally, at least. The night before, he told the dog to wake him up if the deer came. Our trusty watchdog slept through the whole night raid less than 20 feet away.

One year, the deer trimmed up the ivy on our big maple. A perfectly straight line about six feet high separated the ivy from the bare trunk with wooded vines beneath. My sister-in-law asked how I got it trimmed so neatly. I told her it was easy. Actually, I slept through the entire process.

If you live near woods, or even if you don't, you've probably seen deer in your yard. During bad years, they move closer and closer to cities and people in search of food. They can be quite destructive, especially when they rake their antlers on small trees, which often don't survive. Several of my medium-sized pine trees have looked as if a chain saw went up the trunk sideways, eating bark as it went. Deer do much more damage in a year when their food supply is limited as after a heavy snowfall, or in a very dry year like this one.

So what can you do to protect your expensive shrubbery? You can plant things they don't like. My book says they won't eat ivy, but the deer didn't read it. You can buy expensive gadgets to foil them. I'd like to try one that uses a motion detector to spray water on an intruder. That way my husband could pick his breakfast blueberries and have his shower at the same time.

You can try to fence them out. From an upstairs window, I once watched a deer standing beside an 8 foot chain link fence, with barbed wire on top, that separated her from a beautiful pasture. Soon she leapt completely over the fence, from a standing start. Even Michael Jordan couldn't do that. Maybe.

You can use spray to discourage them. Many types are available. I bought a pepper spray that makes even ivy taste bad to the deer. It works, sort of like putting garlic on ice cream. The only drawback is that you have to reapply after every rain. Last winter, I idly commented that we should probably spray the ivy. Neither of us did, and next morning the ivy was again neatly trimmed.

On the other hand, you can ignore it and enjoy the fact that wildlife finds your place attractive. If they like it, probably people do, too.

FRUITS - THE PERENNIAL HARVEST

When I was young and energetic, I read about people who chucked the good life and moved to the country, where they became totally independent. They raised goats and cattle, grew their own food and made everything by hand. I admired this, and for a time I dabbled at the independent life. On our five acres, we raised chickens, geese, ducks, horses, pigs, steer, and sheep, though not all at once. Luckily, we kept our day jobs, because there were some difficult times.

Trying to keep ducks in your own yard is not a simple task. The sheep were a delight to watch, but were easy prey to roaming dogs. Goats were entertaining, but like to kill trees by eating the bark. My pilgrim geese raised babies and grew huge. One Christmas dinner was very slim when I had a goose butchered for our dinner. Too late, I discovered they are mostly bone and cavity. On the other hand, one goose egg can serve an entire family for breakfast.

The last time our steer got loose (my husband was out of town), he scared my son and I by twirling us around on a rope crack-the-whip fashion until all three of us fell to our knees. The next day, he went to the butcher, and that was the end of my farming period.

What has endured? My desire for self-sufficiency is now satisfied by fruit. The blueberries that we planted produced fruit for well over twenty years before having to be replaced. Blueberries are attractive shrubs with delicate white flowers in the spring. Though the rhubarb and peach trees succumbed long ago, we are again trying strawberries and grapes. There's nothing more satisfying than walking out in your back yard to pick fruit for your breakfast cereal. But even that satisfaction can't compare with the taste of fresh-picked fruit ripened where it's eaten. You know what chemicals have or have not been used, and you are solely responsible for the cultivation and harvest.

There are many fruits easily grown in this area. Some fruits, like raspberries and blackberries, don't ship or keep well, and so are seldom found in stores. You can grow these at home, but don't let them take over your back yard.

Rhubarb is another good grower, and it responds well to compost and acid soil. My mother-in-law once struggled to have a good crop of rhubarb without much luck. Someone told her to put her tomato peels from canning on the rhubarb, and it responded beautifully. Probably the acid and the organic matter improved the soil to the rhubarb"s liking. Rhubarb produces for years, properly kept. I can still taste my grandma's strawberry and rhubarb pies.

Grapes are easily grown in Ohio, and are prolific. You have to be ready to prune them back hard, or they produce more leaves and vines than fruit. Been there, done that. This time we planted three seedless varieties, and they're already growing on the wires we provided. We are pruning each plant to four main branches. You can propagate grapes easily by layering, or sticking the middle part of a branch into the soil until it roots, and then cutting it away from the original plant.

Fruit trees offer long-term production from one plant. Many varieties grow well in this area, and your local nursery can give you advice. Nut trees are another possibility, but you have to be ready to pick up under them, or plant them where the squirrels will do it for you.

If you plant fruit perennials, you might want to think about the long time between harvest and the massive harvest when it comes. Are you prepared to can, freeze, dehydrate or make a lot of jelly when the fruit comes in? If you aren't, you can always invite friends in to share the bounty, give it to a food pantry or senior center, or let the birds and wildlife do their thing.

Fruit is low fat, zero cholesterol, and loaded with vitamins and nutrients. Grown on your own land, it's also low cost. Why not use your hard-earned property to reduce your grocery bill?

TREES — NATURE'S PANACEA

A long time ago, I made myself a promise to plant to least one tree a year. Trees add greatly to the value of a home. They are the "bones" in the landscape design, permanent centers of planting beds or interest. I cringe when I see new homes with no trees planted. Many years pass before the lot looks lived in.

Trees reduce cooling costs for the home. They use carbon dioxide to grow, and produce oxygen in return. Highway departments have begun to plant them along freeways. They absorb noise. They soften harsh lines of a home. They offer places to climb, tie a swing, or contemplate. They collect dust on their leaves, and drop it to the soil in rain. In the fall, they fertilize the soil by returning their leaves and needles to decompose. Move those to a compost pile! They provide shade on a hot day. Some trees bear fruit or nuts, and many have flowers in season. In the fall, people take trips to see their magnificent color.

Trees offer "Vacancy" signs to wildlife. Squirrels love to jump from branch to branch and build their sloppy nests high, while birds build tight circle ones in the crook of a branch. If you don't have trees, you probably won't have many birds on your property. And who would want to live where birds don't sing you awake?

Trees can designate an event or memorialize a person. We bought a flowering crabapple for our friends' fiftieth wedding anniversary. They've moved it twice, and it's still going strong. Our first Christmas here we bought a balled and burlapped white pine as a Christmas tree, and later planted it outside. That tree is now about thirty feet tall. Planting our Christmas trees became a tradition.

Planting a tree is a big decision. Because they are slow growers, it takes years before you realize your mistake. Our weeping willow was easy to start by sticking a branch in the soil, and grew very fast. But its roots stuck out of the ground and were impossible to mow over. It left a stump four feet across when we removed it.

Two silver maples tended to break and split during storms or under heavy ice or snow. Since they were both close to the house, we decided to remove them. Some consider them a nuisance tree.

Some we simply planted in the wrong place, far too close to the house, and these were beginning to cause moss and other problems on the roof. These had to go, too.

We planted one by the road directly under the power lines, and it blocked our view as we exited the driveway, a fact that almost caused an accident a few years ago when a car decided to pass just behind the tree as I was pulling out. After that, we limbed it up (trimmed the lower branches), which helped, but didn't solve the problem, so we removed it too.

We still have heavy shade in our yard, and plenty of trees. Three oak trees are growing very straight and tall, but slowly, as trees do. The buckeye tree, planted in honor of our beloved Ohio State University Buckeyes, looks promising. A redbud moved from the woods is looking clever in its corner. This year I planted two small Gingko trees, and look forward to seeing them mature.

The best time to plant a tree is fall. They have time to settle in before winter, and can grow roots all winter before supporting growth in the spring. Nothing is as beautiful as a golden red tree in October. Pick out a small one and plant it this September. You'll be glad you did.

MUMS COME BACK NEXT YEAR

You don't have to be a gardener to grow mums. You just go to a nursery, look over row upon row of perfectly grown potted mums, and agonize over the color palette decision. Then you take them home, stick them in the ground and throw them away at the end of the season. At least that's what I always did.

This year is the first year that I can say that I have wintered over several mums successfully. My first attempt many years ago at planting a mum from the florist brought not a stem of a mum the second season. Now I realize I had probably purchased a mum that wasn't hardy through the winter and was never intended to grow again.

I, however, took it as a challenge. Mums now lead 18 to 1. That's 18 years the mums fail to look gorgeous the second year. Those years I always got a few straggle stems that looked so poor they were probably embarrassed to flower.

This year I have tightly-formed clumps loaded with buds. This year they are going to be perfect, by all indications. What did I do differently? Well, I paid attention to the directions, not something I'm known for.

Obviously, I made sure I had a hardy variety after that first escapade. Now I have learned that once a flower is forced (made to bloom before its normal time as a florist may do), it is not likely to grow or bloom again.

Second, my years of mulching have produced soil that mums apparently like, and that most plants apparently like. That's, after all, why I do it.

Third, there's a secret to managing this. (This is your reward for reading this far.) The real secret is to pinch out the tops of the stems after they have grown about 6 to 9 inches tall. I know - it sounds simple, but it works. Do this in the spring when they are green and healthy looking, and you really don't want to do it. I didn't until this year. That's why my mums never amounted to much.

"Pinching" is a gardener's term that's not anything like the pinching like you do on St. Patrick's day when someone doesn't wear green. It means to cut out or "pinch" off the top of each stem, which forces more growth out the side of the stems (lateral branching, technically). This is the same concept that you use in pruning to fill out a shrub by pruning the tip of each branch.

So, the past 18 Mays, I would thrill to the sign of the mums beginning to reach for the sky. But in June and July, I would watch them get lean and lanky and finally fall over.

This year in May when the rest of you were lounging around planting impatiens and marigolds, I was taking to pruning the mums. I confess I didn't want to. I felt like a traitor. It seemed cruel. I was probably cutting off a flower bud. I was probably guaranteeing failure. But wait a minute! I certainly hadn't done very well in the past, so it wasn't likely it could be worse. Might as well try.

I'm here to tell you that it worked like a charm. I have thick basketball-size clumps of mums loaded with yellow, burgundy, and white just like (almost) those in the nursery. You can, too.

So as not to rest on my laurels, this year after they bloom, I'll probably divide them and move them around the garden for next year. That way, I'll have even more mums to brag about in the new century. You won't be tired of hearing about it, will you?

LANDSCAPING ACCENTUATES YOUR HOME

Would you like to make a $1,000 investment in your home that would add greatly to its resale value? Even better, one whose value would increase over time?

Real estate agents call a home that is easy to sell is one that has "curb appeal," a major factor in which is the landscaping around the house. It is the landscaping that softens or accentuates the lines of the house. It is the landscaping that creates a pleasing entryway, for both drivers and pedestrians. It is the landscaping that adds color, texture and fragrance and changes with the seasons. It is the landscaping.

You may say that I am biased. You're right. But if you don't believe me, take a slow drive around your neighborhood soon. Which houses are most appealing, and why? Which ones are barren, or awkwardly planted, or even overgrown?

Imagine a small white ranch-style home with four overgrown Taxus Yews aligned like soldiers across the front. The shrubs are four feet tall, green prickly tufts at the top, with two feet of bare trunks below. The hardpacked earth is spotted with a few dandelions, and the rain has splashed a haze or reddish-brown mud on the white siding. Steps to the front door protrude nakedly forward. The lawn is patchy, with weeds and worn spots equally represented, and toys scattered about. Two trees in the yard have attained a mature size, but bear lawnmower scars and tufts of grass against their base, marring their dignity.

Now imagine a curving bed with an ornamental tree off the corner, a few shrubs and perennials covering the sharp angles, some mums for color, and a beautiful dark brown or black hardwood mulch protecting the soil from drought, hard rains, and weak seeds. Add a couple of lawn treatments a year, and an appealing play area in the rear for the kids, and you have a vastly improved home for resale - and for quality of life.

It doesn't take a lot of money to landscape your home. It does take some intelligent planning or advice, and that is often free if you agree to purchase the plants from a nursery center that provides it. You can reduce the cost of landscaping by doing some or all of the installation yourself. You can also buy small plants and let them mature on your property for free, rather than in the nursery's holding beds.

There's still time this fall to make these changes. By spring, if you do, your plants will be stretching out in their new home. In three years, they will look as if they have always been there. Best of all, the day after the landscaping has been installed, you will enjoy it every time you come home.

CLEAN UP OR WISH YOU HAD

So - you are starting your annual exercise regimen. I know, because this is when I begin every year. May I make a suggestion? If you want to stretch those muscles a little before you start pounding them on the pavement or the Nautilus machines, you might use them to clean out those flower beds and garden rows.

It's a good time, before the snow piles up on all the debris and provides a wonderful home for insects and diseases for the winter. Also, the leaves will be coming down in a week or two and demanding your attention.

If you have an extra hour or two this week, take a bucket or a wheelbarrow, some gloves, pruning shears or a knife, and walk around your property. Cut off any annual flowers at ground levels or pull the root ball right out of the ground and throw it in the bucket.

Dandelions, crabgrass, or other weeds can go in the bucket too. Perennials' dead flower heads should be removed, but not the leaves. Some perennials add structure throughout the winter, and give you something to look at in that barren month of February. Regardless, they are building strength through their leaves for next year. Leave them alone.

If they don't, usually the leaves collapse after the first killing frost and form their own natural mulch for the winter. Nature has a way of providing for herself. Hosta, for example, eventually dies back to the ground level. The leaf stems, however, have an annoying habit of sticking up all winter and looking brown and ugly. I should cut them off, but I want them to be there to build strength for next year. I know - I've tried leaving them. I will be cutting back sage, irises, sedum, geraniums, and all annuals. I will leave the mums till later, which probably means I won't cut them back till spring. Some plants that are flowering - baby's breath, for example - can be dried and used in arrangements for the winter.

I used to think that leaving the plants would trap leaves for the winter, and thus provide natural mulch for the plants. While this is technically true, it is also true that wet, technically soggy, packed whole leaves mat down and form an almost impenetrable barrier for spring plants. They also don't rot well, because the air can't penetrate them. For years, I couldn't understand why my pachysandra didn't want to spread in certain areas. Eventually, I figured out that it was the oak leaves that were falling there and getting trapped between the plants. Oak leaves are very sturdy and long-lasting.

They were still there in the spring and the pachysandra wasn't. When we began to lightly rake them out early in the spring or fall, the pachysandra rebounded. So, leaves are best removed from flower beds, and a gentle motion with a rake will usually do the trick. If the leaves are shredded and returned to the beds, they are a great benefit to the soil and the plants.

As I make my rounds this week, I will be looking for plants that didn't do well this summer, or are not in a good location. I will either move or discard them. I have several that were not good placements or plant choices in the first place, and this is an easy time to pull them out. The ground is very soft and forgiving from all the rain.

One of my ground covers is taking over a flower bed, and I am considering removing it, but am not looking forward to the task. It has totally filled the bed, and the other plants have lost their focus because of the ground cover. On the other hand, I don't have to mulch the bed since the ground cover is so thorough. Maybe I'll leave it another year. The ground cover is Sweet Woodruff, a very pretty little leafed plant that I understand makes a great potpourri when dried. Perhaps I'll try that this year before I decide to remove it.

Quiz for the day: Where do we put all the stuff we collect in our bucket? RIGHT! The COMPOST PILE!!!

Fall cleanup is a great time to smell that sparkling air freed of pollen and humidity, get those muscles warmed up for the leaf raking time, and make those planting areas look tidy all winter. The best part is the way you'll feel when you're finished, proud of a job well done.

NEED REJUVENATION?

Lately, I've been feeling the need for rejuvenation. It usually happens in September. I look out at my overgrown flower beds and think, "Why did I plant all that stuff?" I've enjoyed cutting flowers and filling vases in my house for several months now, but the last two weeks of heat have finally brought out the doldrums in my flowers.

Nothing is so unattractive as brown-spotted foliage and droopy seed heads. (But you might want to save a few of these.)

So, this morning, out I went in the middle of a rain shower to chop some things down. First went the Zinnias.

There were dandelions underneath, and out they went, too. I will replace these with mums for the fall. Best of all, behind the zinnias I found three beautiful dark red dahlias in full bloom, hidden from view. I cut two and put them in a tall vase with clear marbles.

After I got started, I was unstoppable. I cut down all the zinnias, plus two unnamed plants that I bought two years ago from a catalog. They had not added much to the view, and I didn't like their floppy habit and dog-eared look after blooming, so out they went.

Then I noticed my goldfish pond. This year, I added more plants to it, having had success in the past in keeping the water clear when there were enough plants to shade it. However, the feather plant (parrot feather) that looked gorgeous creeping across the pond last spring had completely covered it and was edging out of the pond into the flower beds.

The fish were invisible beneath it. Once I started pulling these out, it became a compulsion. Even the oxygenator plants beneath were also solid in the water.

Another tall potted plant in the pond had actually sent out three new plants, one on each side of the pond. These had traversed the pond and then sent roots down and a new plant above the water, with no soil to support it.

I had assumed this plant would be ladylike and not colonize my pond - wrong. I removed the three small plants but not the mother pot. I probably will discard it after the first frost. These aggressive plants were choking the water lilies out. If I let this continue, my fish would not have a place to swim for all the greenery and roots.

Nearby, I saw that my redbud tree branches, neatly pruned last spring, were again drooping down over the strawberry plants, so I removed another level of lower branches. I looked up the hill and realized the fencerow was choked with small trees and shrubs, and our view to the top would soon be blocked.

We needed to open up a window in the fencerow to be able to see the deer cross every evening and the mist in the morning. Hopefully, Jim would do this.

Yesterday, I organized my nursery bed getting ready for the winter. I moved about 30 pots of boxwood shrubs propagated two years ago into a line between our front and back yards. They were small but healthy. I hoped putting them into the soil would rejuvenate them and give them better protection from the winter cold with their roots tucked into the earth. Jim came home while I was moving plants and planted and mulched all of them. Bless his heart. I am looking forward to watching these mature into a low hedge. They are slow, compact growers, so not much trimming should be necessary for many years.

When we moved here, I began to plant things that would come up year after year so as to gradually fill the landscape. We did that for many years until the kids were teens and our time was filled up with their activities. After they went to college, my love of gardening again had time to grow, and so did the plants. Now our problem years later is rejuvenation.

While some plants have a very long life, as in trees that may live hundreds of years, others need help along the way if they are to continue. Planting things and forgetting them is a recipe to a jungle landscape. Often trimming and cutting make a huge difference in the health of a plant. Sometimes, a heavy hand with an ax is the best solution, and a trip to the nursery to replace it.

Jim came out while I was a whirling dervish in the flowerbed, and crept up the hill, saying he had to work on the barn. He still has blisters from planting the boxwood yesterday. I guess I'd better not ask about the fence row right now.

ENGLISH GARDENS NOT FOR ME

Have you noticed a hierarchy of nations when it comes to gardening? Think about it. Which country is known for its gardening ability? Right. Great Britain has a reputation for gardening. They are known for developing the Cottage Garden style, which consists of wide beds around the house and in the borders, all chock full of beautiful flowers. Did you ever notice that here we have weather, while in England they have climate?

A few years ago, I subscribed to a gardening magazine because I thought it would teach me some of the things I needed to learn. I was disappointed to learn that it was over my head, since it used a lot of scientific names for plants that I didn't recognize, and that all the pictures were from gardens in England. I was a little resentful, I'll admit.

When it came time to renew, I didn't, and eventually that phone call came wanting to know if I wanted to renew. I said no, and he asked why. Honesty has never been a problem with me, and it wasn't that day. I said it was over my head because of all the scientific names that I didn't know.

"Well, isn't that a good way to learn?" I supposed so, but how could I learn them when they didn't give the common names as well? Also, all the pictures were from English gardens.

"But they are the experts in gardening, aren't they?" I allowed as how they might be, but I didn't know what the climate was, and certainly there were a few gardens in America worthy of pictures. He said they were working on the magazine and he'd appreciate my giving it another try to see if it got better. Amazingly, soon American gardens were beautifully portrayed in the magazine, and common names were given along with the scientific names of plants. He was right - I am learning some names from this magazine. I'm still subscribing, so we both got what we wanted.

There is a national style of gardening that develops, though this is a big country and represents many different planting zones and weathers. As I give plants to my relatives, I realize just how big this country is. From Florida to northern Indiana is a big difference, and many plants won't go either place. Interestingly, some will, and I've just had to discover those with a little research.

Years ago, we visited the Netherlands, and I was fascinated with the tiny gardens the homes had there. They literally have pulled the sea back and pumped it out, so land is a precious commodity there. I saw tiny lawns sometimes ten feet square, with flowers and plants tucked in every square inch. From the train, I saw the chain link fence which separated a private lawn from the railroad property. The homeowner, I presume, had climbed the fence and planted flowers and vegetables on the railroad property for us all to enjoy.

A friend who spent most of her life on Long Island in New York once told me that there, people planted every square inch they could. Here, she said, people have huge lawns and don't plant as many things. She's right. I looked at my lawn with a new eye that day, And I gradually began to make flower beds to connect trees and other obstacles. As I did, I saw that it simplified the lines and improved the look of the lawn as well.

So - I am over my resentment of Englishmen, I think. Someday I would like to visit, just to satisfy my curiosity, but I'm not a cottage garden person. I'm an American gardener, and proud of it.

HARVEST TIME

One of the reasons I love gardening is its similarity to life itself. A gardener knows, through long experience, that preparation of the soil is critical to the success of the plant. A gardener knows that whatever he or she sows, that's what will come up, with a few weeds thrown in for good measure. A gardener knows that the care taken during the process will help ensure a good result at the end of the season. Finally, a gardener knows that sometimes, even with all the care and preparation, a little luck with the weather can change it all

My Ohio Master Gardener newsletter came this week, and Marianne Riofrio, State Master Gardener Coordinator, asked us to make time to think about our "harvest" - our accomplishments - this year. Have we done the things we set out to do? When I look at my garden, it's easy to see those things that didn't work, and maybe to determine the cause. In life, it's sometimes not so easy. Ms. Riofrio suggests that we write down both the things that went well and the things that didn't. It is this constant rite that may improve our gardening - and our life.

Enough philosophy. Things I heard recently from people: "My apple tree doesn't do very well. I probably should spray it, huh?"

"Have you pruned it?" Silence.

"Well, not for a long time. We had a guy do it once, but it's really thick now. Should I have it done again?"

"You'd probably have a lot nicer harvest." I should have told her that a robin should be able to fly through it, but I restrained myself.

Another question: "Mums don't come back, do they?"

"Yes, if they are the hardy type. Some places sell non-hardy types for a one season burst of color. Florist mums usually don't come back because they're not designed to." Nothing is prettier amongst scatter falling leaves than brightly colored mums, whether hardy or non-hardy.

Last week, Jim and I installed some landscaping for friends, starting from scratch. What a pleasure to pile up clean, pure topsoil into whatever shape we needed, and to put brand new beautiful plants inside. They drew up lawn chairs and watched as we worked. It made me want to go back home and start removing things from two of my beds which have become cluttered over the years. I keep saying that, but haven't tackled it yet.

The next task on my mind, though, is raking the leaves. We used to really enjoy raking leaves and appreciated the exercise. For some reason, I can't think why, it's become a lot more work than it used to be. We are looking into buying a leaf vacuum for our mower this year. I will enjoy using it during halftime of the Ohio State Buckeye's games. I plan to be on the mower, and hopefully, Jim can be convinced to be the emptier of chopped leaves into the garden. I'll be pondering the seasons of life as we work. (Note: We never did buy the leaf vacuum. Still raking.)

Happy harvest time.

PRESERVE THE BOUNTY

Many of you have gardens that are bursting right now. What you can't eat each day can be enjoyed all year round by preserving. The same benefits you enjoy during the growing season - taste, vitamins, freshness, and quality - can be enjoyed in January as well as August.

I know. You don't have time to do that. However, a couple of hours away from the television per week can be enough. You'll get more exercise and fresh air that way, and there's nothing like seeing a row of beautiful jars filled with food grown, harvested and preserved with your own hands to produce a feeling of accomplishment and pride. The kids and spouse can help, and you can have a good talk while you work.

I use three methods to preserve food: freezing, canning, and dehydrating or drying. Of the three, drying is the least work. I find canning the most satisfying, and freezing the quickest. I like using my pressure canner because the jars are spotlessly clean and seal almost immediately when they come out. The jiggling noise is impressive too.

You need a certain amount of equipment for any of these processes, but freezing requires the least.

For dehydrating, I use a machine, though it's not necessary. You can use your oven or make your own solar type. You can dry tomatoes, fruits, and even meat safely. The machine uses a small amount of electricity and holds several trays of food at once. You rotate the trays occasionally over a day and a half or so to complete the process. Large foods like apples or peaches must be sliced, cored, or seeded before drying. We often take dried apples on bike rides for a mid-trip snack. Dried pineapple chunks or slices are better than candy. Other fruits, like blueberries or cranberries, can be dried whole, though they may fall through the grid of the dehydrator as they get smaller. You can dry herbs or flowers and your kitchen smells wonderful.

My husband loves beef jerky, and we have tried this a few times, too. In fact, he loves it so much that he does it himself. I oblige by helping him consume them.

You can make your own potpourri from your flowers and herbs. If you've ever bought those at the store, you know how much they cost. Yours are much cheaper and much more rewarding.

Freezing doesn't require a lot of special equipment, just large pans, bowls, colanders, spoons, and plenty of ice. I use a pan of boiling water on the stove, a bowl of cold water with ice cubes nearby on the counter, a colander inside another bowl. I dump the blanched (boiled briefly) food directly into the colander in the ice water bowl for the chilling process. Then I remove the colander to another pan for draining and packaging. I use plastic bags for freezing most things except liquids, and for those I use plastic containers.

Canning probably requires the most equipment. I have a large pressure canner, and large enamel pot for hot pack canning, a jar holder for lifting hot jars, a couple of wide-mouth funnels for filling jars, numerous large pots for miscellaneous processing, a blender for pureeing, and many jars and lids. My first canning book was the Ball Blue Book, available by mailing to that company, and often available in grocery stores during the summer season. The address for the company is on the box of canning lids or jars, I believe, or from their website. It lists the various safe times for canning each different product, and also covers freezing, too. Of course, they recommend you use Ball canning jars for freezing, and I sometimes do. My new favorite book about preserving food is called "Stocking Up", by Carol Hupping and the staff of the Rodale food Center. This one covers all the methods I've discussed here, and many more. A word of caution here: follow directions for preserving your food. If you don't, or if you try a shortcut, you are at the very least losing some vitamins, and at the very worst endangering your family's lives. Neither one is worth experimenting for me. Note: I have canned for years and haven't once caused someone to be sick. Just follow the directions.

My favorite canning project is tomato juice or sauce. I put lots of spices in it, and boil it down as long as I can, and that determines its thickness. I use this in soups and stews and sauces all year long. We also sometimes buy produce like fruit and preserve it. I know exactly what has been used, and I can make sauces without sugar if I like. I love adding home preserved items to my Christmas or New Year's dinner, because it reminds me of my summer garden.

No 79 cent can of peaches bought from the store can give me the same feeling of pride as these.

REJUVENATING: GOOD FOR YOUR GARDEN

Lately I've been feeling the need for rejuvenation. It usually happens about this time of year. I look out at my overgrown flower beds and think, "Why did I plant all that stuff?" I've enjoyed cutting flowers and filling vases in my house for several months now, but the last two weeks of heat have finally brought out the doldrums in my flowers. Nothing is so unattractive as brown-spotted foliage and droopy seed heads.

So this morning, out I went in the middle of a shower to chop some things down. I love working in the rain, a cooling mist. Out first went the Zinnias. There were dandelions underneath, and out they went, too. I will replace this area with mums for the fall. Best of all, behind the zinnias I found three beautiful dark red dahlias in full bloom, hidden from view. I cut two and put them in a tall vase with clear marbles.

After I got started, I was unstoppable. First the Zinnias. I found two unnamed plants that I bought two years ago from a catalog. They had not added much to the view, and I didn't like their floppy habit and dog-eared look after blooming, so out they went. Then I noticed my goldfish pond. This year I added more plants to it, having had success in the past in keeping the water clear when there were enough plants to shade it. However, the feathery plant (parrot feather?) that looked gorgeous creeping across the pond last spring had completely covered it and was edging out of the pond into the flower beds. The fish were invisible beneath it. Once I started pulling these out, it became a compulsion. Even the oxygenator plants under the water were almost solid. Another tall potted plant in the pond had actually sent out three new plants, one on each side of the pond. These had traversed the pond and then sent roots down and a new plant above the water, with no soil to support it. I had assumed this plant would be ladylike and not colonize my pond - wrong. I removed the three small plants, but not the mother pot. I probably will discard it after the first frost. These aggressive plants were choking the water lilies out. If I let this continue, my fish wouldn't have a place to swim for all the greenery and roots.

Nearby, I saw that my redbud tree branches, neatly pruned last spring, were again drooping down over the strawberry plants, so I removed another level of lower branches. I looked up the hill and realized that the fencerow was choked with small trees and shrubs, and our view to the top would soon be blocked. We needed to open up a window in the fencerow to be able to see the deer cross every evening and the mist in the morning. Hopefully, Jim would do this.

Yesterday I organized my nursery bed getting ready for the winter. I moved about thirty pots of boxwood shrubs propagated two years ago into a line between our front and back yards. They were small but healthy. I hoped that putting them into the soil would rejuvenate them and give them better protection from the winter cold with their roots tucked into the earth. Jim came home while I was mowing and planted and mulched all of them. I am looking forward to watching these mature into a low hedge. They are slow compact growers, so not much trimming should be necessary for many years.

When we moved here, I began to plant things that would come up year after year so as to gradually fill the landscape. We did that for many years until the kids were teens and our time was filled up with their activities. After they went to college, my love of gardening again had time to blossom and grow, and so did the plants. Now our problem years later is rejuvenation.

While some plants have a very long life, as in trees that may live several decades, others need help along the way if they are to continue. Planting things and forgetting them is a recipe to a jungle landscape. Trimming and cutting make a huge difference in the health of a plant. Sometimes dividing and replanting is the answer. Sometimes a heavy hand with an axe is the best solution, and a trip to the nursery to replace it.

Jim came out while I was a whirling dervish at the flower bed, and crept up the hill, saying he had to work on the barn. He still has blisters from planting the boxwood yesterday. I guess I'd better not ask about the fence row right now….

SNOW PACKED WITH
GARDEN PRODUCTS

February thoughts usually bring to mind cold, snow, and hearts for Valentine's Day. But with so much happening at winter's annual flower shows, you'll be sure to be thinking spades, decks, and garden clubs.

We found the show to be jam-packed with acres of majestic gardens, new homes, educational seminars, and hundreds of exhibitors showcasing the latest home and gardening products.

A German castle met us at the entrance, and led us inside where we were greeted by trees and plants in full leaf and flower, defying the laws of nature. We found ourselves in what appeared to be a small German village, complete with patios, window boxes and red and white checked gingham tablecloths. I was pleased to see my favorite hydrangeas there, along with tulips, hollies, hyacinths, boxwood and evergreens. Spring was inside.

There were many water features, moats and bridges, all on the theme of "Discover Deutchland", a tribute to Germany.

Once we "oohed" and "aahed" our way through the gardens, we found the exhibitor's booths, where I immediately purchased a small statuette, guaranteed Ohio winter-proof and lightweight. After the first ten minutes, though, I decided it wasn't so lightweight after all. My next purchase was a copper ladybug that dances on a spring in the breezes. I hoped it would develop a patina with age.

I dreamed over the weathervanes, the copper watering sculptures, the pond statues, and even the all new digital piano. I petted a Humane Society puppy, which made us both smile. We sat on lawn mowers, in cars and atop a tall teakwood chair, where the salesman said I looked great, but I already knew that trick.

We tested windows and doors, sat in a gazebo and tasted cooking samples. We watched filthy carpets come magically clean. We tried new loppers that ratchet the branch in two, instead of asking muscles to match brute strength against nature's design. We watched cooking, sewing, craft, woodworking, and dog obedience demonstrations. We saw young men demonstrating ab-building machines. We visited booths for lawn ornaments, plant accessories, and garlic. Jim tasted chicken, peanut brittle, and anything edible, often returning for seconds. A brown boxer dog and his owner came by, and my finger touched his nose as he passed. The boxer's I mean.

I admired many plants and discovered one that I've coveted in the pages of magazines. This curly version of a cypress has a lacy texture that reminds me of my grandmother's starched lace doilies. The label identified it as a Hindi Cypress "Gracilius Nana". Garden centers, take note. I'll be looking for this one. Often in a Home and Garden show, the home part overwhelms the gardening part, but the Cleveland show makes a valiant attempt to equalize the two.

The best part was seeing green. It's been a long time.

USE WINTER WISELY FOR
SPECIAL PROJECTS

I met a man who reminded me of my husband this weekend. He was working on a project in his garage this winter. Scattered about on the floor lay several long tree branches, hooked together rather haphazardly. He apologized for his appearance several times, saying that he was hoping to create an arbor for his perennial bed, but somehow it had fallen on him in the process. He had a huge black eye and a swollen left cheek. I hope he can think of an exciting story as to how it got there.

I have been dropping hints to my husband about creating some rustic furniture out of the plentiful woods we have on our property. So far, he has been successful in ignoring those hints. I have visions of benches on the hillside, tucked neatly under the trees to provide places to ponder the existence of man in peace with nature. Lately, I have to do this on the lawn mower, which loses something in the peaceful part.

Since we will be spending a lot of time inside this winter, I've been thinking about ways to keep my gardening hand in. I received my seed order from the catalogues, and intend to start Euphorbia, geraniums and several other perennials and annuals in the next two months. Euphorbia, a flowering perennial, should be started soon to allow time to reach flowering stage this summer, so I will brave the elements to get to the greenhouse soon.

Somehow, working inside a humid, sunny greenhouse on a snowy day is its own reward. Many plants, while needing bottom warmth for germination, actually do better in a cool greenhouse after they begin their growth. I tried to select those from the catalogue descriptions, but I'm still learning, so I don't expect perfection. Those things that don't work aren't really failures, just notches on my learning belt.

I have started some cuttings on the propagation bench with heating mats, and look forward to their progress. My tiny boxwood hedge gives me pleasure every time I pull my car into its spot, when I see it peeking above the snow cover. I hope it makes it through till spring. Though it will be three or four years before it's a real hedge, I will enjoy watching its progress.

Thanks to some generous friends who recognize my gardening addiction, I also have an amaryllis plant to watch develop and some paper whites to force for spring. Forcing means developing a plant indoors that normally grows outside. The amaryllis is a bright red, huge flowering plant that grows almost magically once it gets started. Right now, mine has a very small green tip sticking out of the bulb, and every day I check to see if it's taller. So far, it isn't, but once the roots develop these can grow as much as a few inches a day.

The paper whites are a type of Narcissus, similar to daffodils. These are great for forcing (making them bloom out of their season), because they don't require a cold period before they sprout, like the daffodils in your yard do while the record-breaking cold passes overhead. Because they don't need this, they can be purchased at the garden center and immediately planted in a bulb pot for quick sprouting and blooming during winter. Last year, I tried this for the first time with limited success. I think my error was in putting the bulbs too deeply in the stones, where they rotted in the water. They grew, but looked sickly. This year, I noted the successful ones actually sat on top of the stones where their roots could go beneath the stones for water. I will try this soon.

Nothing is more uplifting than something blooming in the house during bleak February, unless it's a Caribbean cruise. Maybe if I don't ask Jim to build some rustic furniture he would consider a cruise!

GOOD SOIL IS THE KEY TO GARDENING

If you're like me, you're beginning to wonder if spring will ever come. But one thing you can think about while you're sitting in the recliner on a long winter's night is the soil that supports every plant in your garden. Healthy plants can more easily withstand diseases and pests. The plants look better and taste better. And isn't that what gardening is about?

So what is the perfect garden soil? That is a loamy, soft soil that contains enough humus (rotted stuff), so that water easily penetrates it and drains away, or percolates through like the water in your coffee grounds. (Used coffee grounds are great to enrich the soil, by the way.)

The soil should be fluffy enough so that air is inside, not packed down tight like our clay soil. For most plants, it should have a pH of about 6.5 to 7.0, or slightly acid. It looks and feels dark and rich.

Remember the last time you took a walk in the woods? Remember that rich musky smell? That loamy soil is doing its thing. What makes it that way? It's all those leaves falling every year, and rotting into the ground. Then the earthworms come along and drag that rich humus deeper and deeper and make that soil soft and pliable to a depth of several inches. Got the idea? It's a matter of adding humus - leaves, compost, mulch, whatever you have - and giving it time. Not a lot to ask for an awesome garden, is it?

So how can you replicate that in your lawn and garden? Well, first of all, don't rake the leaves and take them to the city dump. That way no one benefits from those leaves, because they get packed down with no oxygen and won't rot for many years. Rake them if you want to protect your lawn, but shred them and place them on your flower bed or vegetable garden (sheet composting), or put them in your compost pile to use next year. A huge quantity of leaves will rot down to a very manageable amount after a few months. Composting is the ideal way to get lots of organic material wherever you want it. Put your coffee grounds, banana peels, grass clippings (if you haven't added chemicals) leaves, sawdust, vegetable peels, egg shells, even shredded newsprint (save this column, though). No, compost doesn't smell nor attract pests if done properly.

Mulch is the way I add organic matter to my flower beds. I put hardwood mulch down once or twice a year, and cover any bare soil with 2 to 3 inches of it. After a year or less, it breaks down, reduces weeds, conserves moisture, and helps to prevent soil runoff in heavy rains. It even looks better than bare soil. When I first started mulching, our ground was so hard it was difficult to put a spade in it. Now in places I have mulched for years, I can usually stick my bare hand into the soil to a depth of several inches. That's loam. That's what the benefits are. I never have to till or hoe for weeds. Any weeds that come up I can easily pull up by hand due to the soft soil.

So while you're sitting in your recliner this winter, pick up the phone and locate a source of clean grass clippings or sawdust or manure or shredded newsprint, and set a date to pick it up this spring. You'll be doing your plants a favor. (PS start to collect green kitchen wastes as well.)

Do compost piles smell? Not at all, unless you put something other than greens in.

COME ON IN - IT'S SPRING INSIDE!

It was bitterly cold with a gusty wind blowing that quickly hurt my face. I hurried inside the Cleveland Home and Garden show. People were everywhere. Babies in strollers, grandmas in wheelchairs, a group of Mennonite ladies in white bonnets. The entrance was beautiful as always - a white vinyl fence and stone wall, red tulips, white rhododendrons and lavender hyacinths. A bed in the center held a rose garden in full bloom. The fragrance was welcome after the cold outside. The fountain splashed a welcome.

I crossed a heavy wooden bridge (available for purchase), over a pond and rowboat, with a log cabin behind. Later, a mannequin bride and groom enjoyed a decorated gazebo. The "bride room" was also for sale. Inspiration was everywhere.

I climbed a stairway of huge flat rocks, unaware of what I was about to see, since it was hidden behind a row of pines. On the way, I passed clumps of teasel, moss, daffodils and a small rustic footbridge over a stream. A white cottage showed off the hydrangeas lining the porch, and a long-haired kitty turned its head as we approached. I gently tapped the cat on its head with my pen. It didn't budge. The lady behind me said, "You just had to check, didn't you?" I had been had.

Eventually, I found my favorite display. A brick courtyard sported a block "O", a Buckeye leaf and a football labeled "National Champions", all in brick. As I got closer, I laughed out loud to see a fountain shooting water directly into a scarlet and gray football helmet. What fun!

Next, a tiny tumbledown shack with a rusty antique tractor backed up a radio announcer who suddenly started to broadcast 2 feet in front of me, live and on the air.

The Ohio Bicentennial exhibit included huge models of the Wright Brothers' biplane, the Marblehead lighthouse, and an Amish horse and buggy, all surrounded by beautiful plants.

A display of white pillars and urns filled with red and white carnations, greenery, small American flags, and surrounded by a border of red cyclamens, focused our patriotism. What pretty plants cyclamen are. And they love the cold weather. They have survived for years in my barely heated greenhouse and still bloom in the cold.

There was something here for everyone: plants, landscaping ideas, remodeling exhibits, hoop games, demonstrations of cooking, gardening tools, wall coverings, statuary, cars, hot tubs, decks, lawn equipment and even clothing. There were seeds, ponds, stone birdbaths, baskets (sorry not Longaberger), bulbs, signs, outdoor lighting, huge floppy insects, herbs, potted plants - endless displays of every gadget a gardener or home decorator could want.

Shows like this are all over the country, I would imagine, and are inspiring, educational, and entertaining. Plants, gadgets, ornaments - all are for sale usually. If you love gardening, find a garden show to try.

LIKE BUCKEYES, CACTI ARE ALSO CHAMPS

I was one of the lucky ones who got to attend the Fiesta Bowl. We made our reservations before OSU beat Michigan, sensing a victory. Finally, the game tickets came through.

In December, I had an interesting discussion with a student who is a Miami fan. I said I thought the Buckeyes had a chance. He said, "No way," that a champion team didn't win like that, so close to the wire. I said it was the coach's style, conservative until he needed a big play. Furthermore, I saw that the Buckeyes just had something that didn't show up on the charts. I didn't name it, but I was thinking heart - and discipline. It was a sense of respect for each other, and determination even when the odds were against them. It was there all season long. It was there to the final seconds of that game in Tempe.

I was sitting there in the second overtime watching the defense between plays, resting their hands of their hips, walking slowly around. "They're tired," I said. "They're beat." For the first time all season, I was afraid they were going to lose. But they didn't. Just a heartbeat away was the play that clinched the game. I gave up, but they didn't.

That team radiates the personality of their coach, Jim Tressel. They are steady as a rock in the face of adversity.

They are true to each other and the goal. That's why I love sports. It's psychology that makes a winner. Lots of athletes have talent. Not many have the internal fortitude to achieve greatness.

During the week, we spent an afternoon with our Arizona relatives at the Desert Botanical Garden in Phoenix. The first of January, it was 75 degrees, with clear blue skies and fresh breezes blowing. Our host said he hoped it rained in January, because then the desert would go into full bloom. The rainfall for a year there is about 2.5 inches. In Ohio, that's a normal rain.

There I saw more cacti than I knew existed. The huge saguaro was everywhere. Next to one was a wooden framework, obviously the interior of a Saguaro. I didn't know that they had a wooden interior. Of course, a plant that large probably needs that structure to withstand desert winds.

Cacti store water in their thick leaves. They are tough, resilient plants, smart enough to adapt to an environment that doesn't help them to survive. They're smart enough to use that to their own benefit. Tough enough to grow in weight and girth by several tons when the rains come, saving that water to use during the many months when there will be no rains. Tough enough to allow birds to chip away nests in their trunks and still grow on.

Tough enough to endure well over 100 degrees day after day without water. Tough enough to plant their roots in sand and gravel and hang on when the tumbleweed gives up and blows away.

They're a lot like the Buckeyes. True champions.

HOLIDAY MOTIVATION FOUND
WHEN SHOPPING

I've done it again. Failed to get motivated for decorating for Christmas until far too late. Today, I made an attempt to rectify that. I got up early and headed out to the nurseries to see the decorations and gardeners' gifts they had beautifully displayed. At an upscale gardeners' shop in Columbus, (these tools never get dirt on them - they're for decorating the house), I saw copper birdhouse ornaments for the tree, square glass vases that turned over to become votive candle holders, leather straps and dog leashes, bulb-forcing kits in fancy colorful bags for gifts, and the end result displayed next to it (mine never look quite that beautiful), of course in a copper pot and saucer.

I didn't buy anything, but I took the motivation with me to the real plant stores right here in Licking County. There, I saw evergreen sprays and mailbox decorations, pine roping, clever ornamental evergreens displayed with red ribbons in a pot small enough to carry up our steps to the living room.

Jim went out last weekend to get a Christmas tree. For years, we have purchased our Christmas trees balled and burlapped ("B and B" in the industry) for planting. Our first Christmas tree in our new home 31 years ago is now about 40 feet tall and beautiful. We were young and strong then, or at least Jim was. This year, he picked out a "small" five foot tree and had two young guys put it in the truck for him. He managed to get it off the truck onto the drive when he got home, and wedged bricks under the ball to keep it upright for a week before bringing it in.

As the week progressed, he began saying things like, "You know, that tree is really heavy. I'm not sure we can get it upstairs. I guess we could put a couple of rods through it to get it up the stairs."

It was beginning to sound not likely that tree would get to the living room. I mentioned we could put it outside on the deck and decorate it there.

"Not have a tree inside?" Mandi sounded disappointed. She, as you may have guessed, is younger than we are. I decided not to mention that one year we actually had no tree at all.

I mused out loud that we didn't even own a tree stand anymore. Jim suggested, as I knew he would, that we could always nail the tree to the floor the way his brother Harold did years ago for their mother's tree. That family story gets told every Christmas. I never liked the tree stand anyway. A tiny bowl filled with water that's easily tipped and spilled as you're moving the tree outside, dry needles dropping all over the floor and a dead tree to get rid of later. Not my idea of environmentally sound. Good business for Ohio, though.

So I went looking this morning for something smaller. One caught my eye. A weeping spruce, tall, thin and in a gallon pot just the size I lug around in the greenhouse all the time, and planted in planting medium rather than one-ton Ohio clay. Of course, it's not three feet wide, but at least it's green, it'll be in the living room and we can handle it. Best of all, it would make a nice addition to the landscape.

Merry Christmas!

EVERY GARDENER HAS CHRISTMAS DREAM LIST

If you're not done with your Christmas shopping and you have a gardener on your list, here are some ideas:

My ten favorite pruning tools for gardeners will make great gifts: bypass loppers, folding pruning saw, quality bypass pruning shears (mine are Felco #2), an extension pruner for reaching high up to the tree without a ladder, dainty and precision scissors for cutting those beautiful bouquets for the house, even a gardener's tool that easily fits in a pocket and can do most small jobs the gardener takes on.

For planting: an English spade (we would call it a fork with flat tines rather than pointy ones), a sturdy rust-proof planting trowel, a light mattock for hand planting potted plants, a ladies' spade (great even for gentlemen) for small jobs, a dibber for planting lots of small plants or bulbs and permanent plant markers for remembering later what it is. All these are handy to have, and store clerks can explain what each is.

For maintenance: a collapsible rake for getting into tight places, a lightweight, easy to use wheelbarrow with two front wheels, garden shoes that you can hose off and slip on, knee pads and various types of trimmers and clippers to keep that lawn looking perfect.

For decorating the landscape: sundials, birdhouses or bird-bath, trellises or arbors, lawn furniture, water garden large or small, gazing ball or statues.

For extending the season: a cold frame, heated seed-starting containers, plant lights or carts with lights for starting quantities of seeds, blooming or green houseplants.

For whiling away the winter hours dreaming of summer gardens: Design books, gift certificates from catalogues or local nurseries, or a garden journal.

You don't have to spend a lot to give your favorite gardener something they will cherish. My young daughter once gave me a certificate that said, "Good for one swingin' in the rain!" I still have it.

WINTER GARDENS CAN BE BEAUTIFUL TOO

A reader wrote to ask: "Any suggestions for a nice fall or winter-blooming shrub or plant? Not mums."

Now in Ohio - a cold zone 5 - there are not very many plants that bloom in winter. Many bloom in the fall, and many have a lot to offer in winter other than blooms. So, let's think about what is applying in winter. (Anyway, what's wrong with mums?)

Shape - Some plants offer interesting structure or shape after the leaves have gone. Harry Lauder Walking Stick is a shrub with twisty twigs that are great to admire in January against the snow. There are also rounded, conical, and pyramid-shaped plants, both evergreen and deciduous, that offer something from the kitchen window on a snowy day.

Texture - Barks, branch type and needles all offer great interest in winter. Take a walk through a park if you want to get ideas for tree and shrub textures. There are some beautiful tan-colored peeling barks that would add to any landscape. Another way to achieve texture is with ornamental grasses. These turn a beautiful golden color (like ripe wheat) and last through winter. The top-heavy plumes catch snow and bend over gracefully, making a very pleasant view for cabin-fevered residents. My miscanthus grass is about five feet tall with 8 inch plumes at the top of each stem. Other grasses are small and compact, and provide a sense of order if planted in groups or lines in the garden.

Some flowering plants develop fascinating seed heads that are attractive in winter: Rudbeckia and echinacea (coneflower) are good examples. You can strip off the flower petals and leave the seed heads through winter. The birds and squirrels will appreciate it, and a little low voltage lighting will accentuate these plants in the long hours of winter darkness. Hydrangeas hold their mophead, panicles, and lace cap offerings through spring. They can also be cut, taken inside and air-dried for long term enjoyment. I have some I dried several years ago, still looking great. The Oakleaf hydrangea offers flowers plus a shaggy bark in winter - a real four-season plant. The River Birch, a tree, has a shaggy bark that exposes different colors of tan as it peels. Related to the Paper Birch, it is much hardier than its cousin, which is susceptible to borers.

Color - Holly offers a bright green shiny leaf that is very appealing in winter, but there are many colors of evergreens such as blue (as in spruce), green (as in boxwood, pine, spruce, etc.) and even gold and yellow varieties of all shapes and sizes.

Berries stay attached well into January and February, depending on how hungry the birds are, and can provide bright color and texture to plantings. Colors include red, yellow, blue, black, and beyond. Be a friend to the wildlife in winter and plant some of these. The red and yellow twig dogwoods are interesting, and winterberry forms a rounded shrub with lots of bright red berries that stay until eaten.

Bones - Bones are anything left after a killing frost that give us structure to the garden, just like our skeletons give us structure. So woody plants and evergreens are important, as are benches, gazing balls, bird feeders and baths, fences, paths, sculpture and hedges between garden "rooms".

Blooms - Yes, there are plants that bloom in winter. The Hellebores do - mine bloomed late winter for the first time last year, and it was very appreciated, too. My heather bloomed early spring, I think, and again later, and has a very soft, green texture all year long. Snowdrops, Winter Jasmine, and Witch Hazel are possibilities as well.

Food - Don't forget that vegetables, well-tended and somewhat protected, can last through the winter: carrots, onions, lettuce and other cold-weather plants can be harvested much of the winter with a little covering. Last year, we took food from the garden for Thanksgiving dinner. Jim had bragging rights for months over that.

Probably the best method of choosing one of these is to take your ideas and your wishes to the nearest nursery and ask. Those professionals know which plants do well in this area, and which don't, and they're not afraid to share what they know. Think about last winter when you hurried inside from cold, and what you saw or didn't see. Winter can be a beautiful time, a time to really see plants. Plan for it, and you will enjoy it far more. I guarantee it.

GETTING READY TO GARDEN

Nothing is a better motivator than getting together with a group of gardeners on a snowy January day to talk about gardening. I did that last weekend at the beautiful Public Library for a free public program presented by Licking County's Master Gardeners. Four presenters talked about their gardens and their knowledge with the hardy group who came. Quite a few attended, considering the weather, and I hope they left as inspired as I did.

The first speaker was brilliant as well as beautiful. (It was me.) I spoke about site analysis, which includes soil analysis, family needs, service areas, preferences, gardening interests, access issues, microclimates, and basic design. Usually we want to jump to the design first, but it pays to do your homework. One of the things we sometimes fail to consider is the family who lives on the site and how they use the property. Hobbies need a place outdoors sometimes, and can range from a tennis court to a chicken coop. Whatever the family's outdoor needs are, whether for recreation, entertaining, or work, they must be taken into consideration when planning a garden.

I reminded folks to plan service areas for trash collection, pets, vegetable gardens, access and views. We discussed what micro-climate means in the home garden, and how you can use it to your advantage. Over time, you will become very familiar with the foibles of your landscape. You will know where all the wet spots, hot spots, frost pockets and favorite dog digging places are. Trust me - it's easier to work around these than to try to change the dog or the weather.

The next speakers wowed the audience with slides of their beautiful gardens in full summer and autumn bloom. Nina Kohser and Chris Lang shared the spotlight as they discussed two different planting philosophies and very different sites. Nina has a small yard packed full of flowers from stem to stern, with a mighty white rose in the center. She calls the rose "madam", as if it is queen of the garden, and the pictures showed that it certainly is. In the small lawn, Nina has carefully selected simple colors for the blooms and concentrated on varieties of foliage texture and shades. The result was beautiful, orderly and peaceful.

Chris Lang has acres to play in on her farm in Licking County. What peaceful vistas she has created and preserved! I almost wanted to be a sheep on her farm just to spend time in the meadow. From her back yard, the land drops away gracefully. Large trees surrounded by plantings provide a foreground for the focal point - the valley below. I could sit all day with a glass of iced tea and watch the winds gently toss the grasses. Another spectacular view is of the trees and daffodils lining her driveway in the spring. It had a natural look but was obviously very well planned. These ladies knew their plants and design.

Last but certainly not least, Tom Beckett shared some of his favorite tools with us. These he had collected from as far away as Zimbabwe and as close as his mother's garage. Tom's love of tools was apparent as he told us about finding some of his treasures at garage sales and pointed out how to identify quality tools. He said to make sure that the metal parts of the tools (a rake, for example) were molded from one piece of metal rather than pieced together, or else the tool would quickly break apart. He also noted the metal straps on some tools like shovels and rakes which go up the handle for extra support and strength. The longer the strap, the stronger the tool.

He also cautioned us to look for a bolt that goes into the handle itself to provide further strength for the tool. He said since he had followed his own advice, even though their tools were more expensive, that someday his grandchildren would be using those tools. Someone in the audience recommended that he give the tools to her, because the grandchildren wouldn't appreciate them. Tom just smiled.

I left the meeting glad I heard the speakers, and I enjoyed it as much as the gardeners in the audience. Now, I am looking forward to spring.

A GARDENER WITHOUT TOOLS IS NOT ONE

If you haven't been motivated to think about gardening during the recent thaw, you probably won't be. The warm breezes and damp earth smells have got my hands itching to start digging. We found a big sale on topsoil and humus, so we bought a pickup truck load and stacked it up in the yard to wait for spring. Before long, it will be frozen solid, and I will be again anxiously awaiting a warm day to start doling it out over the flower beds and garden.

Regardless, spring will come. At least it always has. While you're waiting, take a look at the tools in the shed or the garage, and spend some time getting them ready.

Are the shovels clean, sharp, and oiled? A few minutes sharpening them will save your back in a couple of months.

You can sharpen them on the tip and on the sides if you like, and then put on a fine coat of oil. A cloth dampened with oil will do the job just fine. You can store this in a coffee can in the garage and use it many times. Make sure to keep the lid on tight to prevent fires. Another method is to get a small keg or can, fill it with coarse sand, and then pour a small amount of oil into the sand. Stir it so the sand is evenly and lightly coated with oil. Leave this keg near where the larger tools are kept. When you come in with a shovel freshly used, you can plunge it into the sand, taking off the extra soil by the friction of the sand, and at the same time oiling it.

While you are cleaning, oiling, and sharpening all your shovels, spades, pruners, etc, check the handles for cracks or loose screws. Any cracked handles should be replaced to prevent injury. Check all rake handles and secure them as well. You might want to coat the handles with a light covering of linseed oil to keep them sealed against moisture.

Now get out the cutting tools: loppers, pruning shears, hedge trimmers and so forth, all need to be sharpened and maintained to help you do the job. Oil is the panacea for all tools to prevent rust on metal parts and dry rot of wood handles. Sharpening is critical for these tools for safety and prevention of injury to operator and plant.

Power tools like mowers and chain saws need attention as well. These you might want to take to a professional for cleaning, sharpening, tuning up and general prevention of problems later on in the high season when you really need them. If you usually do it yourself, you don't need me to tell you how.

While you're sorting through the tools, don't be afraid to discard those cheaper models that you bought on sale last year and that have already started to rust or fall apart. A bad tool is a very expensive and dangerous one no matter what the price. Save the space for a good tool.

Storage is an important way to take care of tools as well. Provide a neat way to organize them, and you won't ever come in the garage to trip over a rake. Wall hooks work, as do metal or wood storage boxes with grids at the top for receiving long-handled. tools. These place the top of the tool where it is easily identified, and if the box is tall enough, keeps it from crashing down on your head. Jim prefers hooks or nails or brackets on the wall for most of his, and they are close to the door where it is easy to grab one and go.

We do a lot of that (grabbing and going) after about March. That leaves February for getting ready. An hour or so every weekend can make a huge difference to your tools and your planting season.

GARDENING WORK BEGINS BEFORE SEASON STARTS

All gardeners, UNITE! It's not fair to entice us with that beautiful spring weather only to bring back winter with a vengeance.

I found a couple of ways to beat the winter blues. The Home and Garden Show is in Columbus at the Bricker and Celeste Buildings at the Ohio State Fairground through this weekend. For a $7 ticket, you can meander through paths surrounded by tulips, hyacinths, every kind of water feature you can imagine, and learn about new and old home remodeling ideas.

You can talk with beekeepers, stonemasons, home decorators, mulch experts, landscapers, and fence and deck builders. You can listen to trainings on the stage in the Celeste Building. The best part is just remembering what the summer is like and being inspired for your annual outdoor and indoor projects.

The other method of beating the winter is to visit a greenhouse or park somewhere. I recommend Dawes Arboretum south of Newark, Franklin Park Conservatory in Columbus, Kingwood Center in Mansfield, or if you're up for a weekend, try Longwood Gardens near Philadelphia, PA. If you can't make any of those, try thumbing through your nursery catalogs. If that doesn't do it, you're probably beyond inspiration.

Gardeners are a hardy lot, and usually not afraid to be out and about during the cold snaps. It really makes us appreciate the warmth when it arrives. This week I saw a professional crew trimming thickly branched low trees on a college campus. Three men worked to prune, clean up and supervise the cuts. One tree was finished and a long row awaited their "haircut". The finished tree was much less congested in the middle, and the structure of the tree was obvious to the eye. I didn't envy them their task, as it looked to take the rest of the day at least, but I did envy their work, which took them out into the brisk cold air in pursuit of improving living things along the walk. These trees will be beautiful in the spring, and the men can enjoy them all the more as they remember the cold winds that accompanied their work in February. The trees' blooms will be thicker and healthier than if they had not been trimmed and they will live longer and look better as they do.

My task for this cold day will be to clean out my greenhouse before the spring onslaught of planting begins. For the first time, I shut the greenhouse down in November and left the leftover plants and insects to die in the cold. Now I must remove the used pots, clean up all the areas I can with bleach water to kill bacteria and then spray for insects. In a week or two, I can start my first seeds. My heating bill was a little lighter, but less than I expected, and my worry load was lighter too. I will need to replace the end caps of the greenhouse with new plastic, as the two layers there cannot withstand the solar rays, and one layer has split. We used an old supply to finish the ends, and shouldn't have. The rest of the house is still strong and looks new.

Two benches need work as well. When we built the tables, we covered most of the benches with hardware cloth and two with wooden lath. We didn't know which would work best, but it's obvious now. Five years later, the lath is black with mildew and probably carries diseases. It sags in the middle and threatens collapse any day. It has to go, and I hope Jim can find the time to replace it for me.

His priorities are on his bees right now. During the warm spell we enjoyed, the bees were very active. His mind turned to treating and feeding them before the season begins. Yesterday, he went up to lift the hives to see how heavy they are. That tells him whether they have enough food to finish the winter, or whether he needs to supplement with sugar water on a day above freezing. The bees carry the water inside the hive and use it until spring.

If you see him, would you ask him not to forget my greenhouse benches?

GARDENER FINDS SURPRISES IN SNOW

I skipped going to the gym today. I had a lot to do and decided that I could get some exercise in the yard. It was a very cold day, with bright sunshine and sparkling snow. Good skiing weather, and probably good weather for pruning my clematis vine.

"Pruning?" you say. "Why would you prune in winter?"

I am so glad you asked. Pruning in winter is a great idea. First of all, there's little else to do on a day like this, other than curl up with a cup of tea and a great book. Secondly, in the winter all the leaves are gone, and that allows a great look at the structure of the plant without the distraction of the leaves. You can see which branches are crossing, which are broken and which are going crooked. When you can see them, it's easy to make decisions and easy to get at them to cut.

My Clematis has been on a trellis for quite a few years. When I first planted it, it was so delicate-looking that I left it totally alone for probably five years. Then a few more. This year, though, I noticed that it didn't bloom as much, so I figured it was time for a haircut. The plant is very top-heavy, and we've had to brace the trellis so it doesn't fall over. "A haircut is definitely in order," I thought.

I put on several layers of clothing, dug out an old pair of gloves and heavy boots, found a trash bag for trimmings, strapped on my trusty pruning shears and tool belt, and trudged outside. Our dog Missy was startled to see me there, I think. My black Lab is used to finding me indoors this time of year.

When I arrived at the trellis, I was a little dismayed to see the jumble that had developed while my laissez-faire approach neglected the vine. I tentatively snipped a few branches, the oldest looking ones, but it was so thick it was difficult to get there. Also, once I cut them, I discovered that the tendrils attached one branch to another so it was almost impossible to separate them. Finally, I gave up and chose a sort of "bowl cut". (If you've ever given your son a haircut, you'll know what I mean.) I took out about half of the jumble, and it looks neater, but not natural.

About half-way through this job, I made a discovery. There, snug inside a thick wall of twigs, was a tiny bird's nest. It was laid on several layers of oak leaves to keep out the drafts, I assumed. The nest was of dried reeds, then very small twigs and lastly lined with pine needles. Inside were several acorn caps and shells, remnants of a take-home dinner.

Maybe our feathered friend will appreciate the new growth spurt that will come this spring because of my half-hour of pruning. I hope so. I'll be watching.

Tomorrow, I go to the gym. But the day after that, I will be pruning some of the evergreens on the hill. That will really be a workout.

THE GIFT OF GARDENING

Since I support gardeners everywhere, I have a few hints about gifts for gardeners. I can only tell you what I like, then I'll hope that Santa Claus reads this column, too.

I love gardening books. My first gardening book gave me concepts that have served me well, and it is thoroughly smudged with dirt. Other book ideas are reference books on general gardening, plant propagation, plant lists and characteristics, perennials, specific plants (especially if they're the person's favorite), and how-to books on projects for the garden.

For the houseplant or container gardener, a selection of various pots and sizes would be welcome. Other tools such as moisture sensors, indoor hoses to connect to faucets, watering cans, and plant shelves or display stands would be appreciated.

Outdoor gardeners need supports such as tomato cages, trellises, arbors, and hanging plant brackets. Sculptures or interesting art objects to display in the flowerbeds provide structure, especially during winter. A compost bin, well-used, provides healthy soil to the garden for many years. My favorite (I hope Santa is reading this far) is a garden bench - a joy to look at that also provides a weary gardener a place to enjoy his or her handiwork. A simple flower box can bring the joy of gardening to the elderly, the apartment dweller, or the over-committed yuppie.

Tools are a good choice, too. My philosophy is to buy the best. I learned this after many years of replacing cheap ones. Good tools, well taken care of, last a lifetime. Ideas are pruning shears, loppers, shovels, dibbers, pocketknife, sprinkling cans, cloche jars or boxes, gathering containers, cold frames, propagation tools, grow lights, pruning saws, weed eaters, leaf blowers, potting bench, plant labels - the list is endless. Each of these can add a new dimension to a gardener's expertise and enjoyment. If you don't know what these tools do, drop in to a hardware or gardening store and chat with a clerk.

If you want to give something that won't have to wait until spring, you might try a Bonsai kit, flower of the month, subscription to a birding or gardening magazine, gift certificate from a plant catalogue, or tuition for a class on gardening. If the person is really committed to gardening, you might want to find out about the Master Gardener program through their County Extension Service. Dawes Arboretum (our Newark, Ohio, tree sanctuary) offers many classes on farming and crafts, and their gift shop has some great things for gardeners or nature lovers.

To keep your gardener safe and healthy, you might want to give some protection articles like work gloves, knee pads, rolling seats, sun hats, safety glasses, or boots for the mud, which come in handy, even if not glamorous.

An automatic sprinkling system for the lawn or a greenhouse for the avid gardener will bring you undying gratitude. These don't have to cost a lot if you can do some of it yourself.

All this and I've hardly mentioned plants. You could arrange to have trees, perennials, topsoil, or other planting material delivered in spring. Check with your gardener first. They have their own preferences. Perennials and trees, for example, will increase in value and beauty over the years, and will add to the value of their home.

Gifts that encourage a person to do what they love give far more than the item - they give peace and contentment. Your gardener will be very grateful.

GARDEN CATALOGS

The last few years I've spent New Year's day watching the festivities and football on TV while surrounded by plant catalogs and order forms. It feels like a tradition starting, only a few days later than the arrival of the IRS forms. By New Year's, gardening is looking like fun again. The hot days of July and August are long forgotten, and my pruning shears are itching for a run.

You don't get any garden catalogs? Just subscribe to any gardening magazine. I'll guarantee your mailbox will be overflowing promptly.

Beautiful color photographs entice your eye to what your own garden might look like next spring. They are chock full of information about plants, tools, varieties, and how to grow them. They offer plants not usually available at nurseries, who have to stock for the most common tastes.

Their plants are usually widely purchased and recognized for good reason: they are reliable, attractive, and usually easy to grow. Conversely, those rare and unusual plants in the catalog may have undesirable characteristics or be difficult to grow. You won't know until you try them. That's what I'm doing as I read through these books: deciding whether to try them.

I also learn about myself. For instance, while I like things neat and orderly in my garden, I tend to buy the opposite from catalogs because they look better in the pictures. I'm getting better over the years at selecting and planting things I will enjoy. I learn about what types of plants work best in my yard and where, by reading, choosing, planting and watching. I learn how to use different tools. Mostly I'm able to dream about what I want my garden to look like. I never quite get it there, but it's fun to ponder.

Here are some things you might want to think about as you read catalogs for ideas:

If flowers are pictured in a vase rather than on the actual plant, the plant is probably not very attractive when growing.

If it's described as an "easy spreader", don't buy it unless you can enclose it in concrete. If it "likes full sun", don't try to put it in shade. Just bury the dollar bills instead.

The "Queen of Lilies at a Pauper's Price" is two lies.

"Naturalizing" means you plant it and forget it. This is a wonderful concept when it works.

"Delightful fragrance" means just that. Don't forget this aspect when planting. My viburnum shrub is a real blessing in the spring when its fragrance fills the air for days.

A "squirrel proof" bird feeder isn't. Nothing is.

"Remarkably resistant even in the face of horrendous weather?" Right.

"The clear, vibrant wine-red blooms have a tousled, wild hair kind of look." Who writes this stuff?

"Incorrigibly rambling nature." Don't even think about ordering this one.

"Drought tolerant"- don't plant in that low place in your yard.

Probably the best comment about garden catalogs is one I read recently. They said the best way catalogs can improve your garden is when they are used as mulch.

PESTS KEEP YOU HUMBLE

Two centuries ago when I was in high school, a boy seated in front of me in typing class said he was working on his entomology project. After the teacher told us to be quiet, I wrote him a note: "<u>What</u> is entomology?" In huge letters, he wrote back: "BUGS!" with a smiley face in the "G". His name was Larry, in case he is reading this.

Now is a good time to consider how you will deal with those common garden pests. If you're a gardener, you know about bugs. At the very least, you've seen what they can do to plants. A friend told me that rabbits or deer were eating holes in her Hostas. I told her it was probably slugs, those slimy, disgusting things that climb all over plants in the dark of the night. I understand that if you put salt on them they sort of pop, but I've never had the courage to try.

Last year, my sister-in-law found one of her tomato plants leaning over and wilted as if it had broken off at the base of the stem. Looking closer, she discovered huge green worms on the stems. These were as big as her finger, and a beautiful shade of green that exactly matched the color of the plant. This, I guarantee you, was not a coincidence. She was so startled that she used the only thing she had with her at the time - a piece of string - to "tie up" the worm so she could show it to her son later. Now, I've never known a worm wrangler, but she's coming close. I laughed when she told me later that the worm escaped before her son got home to see it. Later, a little research told me that she had a green tomato hornworm. Did I mention it had horns?

Years later, I took a Monarch butterfly class at our local Dawes Arboretum and I can bet you that "worm" was a baby Monarch. They are huge by worm standards. But they perform huge benefits for our biosystem. When I came home from that class, I found a giant green horned worm on our tomato plant. A few days later, it was gone - flown towards Mexico, I bet. Weeks later we had a Monarch butterfly in our yard.

My other run-ins with pests have included a white cottony stuff on my fuschias (mealy bugs), little green bugs in my greenhouse (aphids), spider mites on my houseplants, raccoons in the birdseed, deer in everything, and my husband in the blueberries. Pests cover a lot of territory, you can see.

Just as a doctor does a balancing act between disease, medication, and side effects, the gardener must determine how important getting rid of the pests is compared to the side effects of the cure.

Chemicals can provide almost instant relief in some cases, but many also eliminate beneficial insects. Later, the problem can return worse than before.

You may decide you need spotless roses - after all, you're entering them in a competition this year, or you plan to make a gift of them to your mother-in-law. On the other hand, you may decide you can live with the lacy effect on the leaves, and you'd rather not have poisons around the house.

Whatever you decide, help is available. Garden centers, books, the internet, and County Extension offices offer help on these and other matters. For almost all of the problems we encounter, solutions are available and effective. It's just a matter of finding one that fits your needs.

If you've been a gardener for long, you've probably figured out that pests are there sometimes because the plant is already weak in some way. Healthy plants are far less susceptible to insect damage than struggling ones. Just one more reason - as if you needed one - to keep your plants healthy and happy.

NEED A NEW HOBBY?

Every day you could be throwing away a valuable resource instead of doing a pubic good by reducing clogged landfills. You could be the envy of all your neighbors. You could be … composting!

I'm talking about rich, black, luxurious compost. Compost is easy to make and great for plants and general soil improvement. All you need is an out of the way spot and the desire. Don't be awed by the contraptions that are sold for hundreds of dollars. You can just pile your garden and kitchen waste in a corner outside somewhere - and wait. But stir while you wait.

No, it's not smelly or slimy or anything bad. It changes texture and colors without your help. Just turn it with a pitchfork a couple of times a week and it progresses. Or get the kids to do it. They may like it.

Anything that was once a growing plant will work: potato peels, apple cores, used coffee grounds and tea bags, pea pods, leftover green beans, dead houseplants, or chopped up fall leaves. You can also use egg shells and shredded newspapers. Some things you should NOT use are meat or dairy scraps, unless you want to attract every dog and rodent in the county. Without those, what you will have is a real, sweet-smelling earthworm factory that breaks down and digests garbage into a crumbly, rich new soil that gradually transforms you soil from clay to loam. Jim has composted for over thirty years and we have never had odor or pest problems with ours. Neither dogs nor deer nor flies have been interested. Worms, yes. Compost needs and benefits by worms.

Find a place on your property that won't offend your neighbors, and keep it neatly raked together. It's not any more offensive than a pile of leaves when neatly done. Other than finding a place, what do you need to know? If you do nothing other than make a pile, it will eventually rot into compost. However, there are a few things that make it a lot more effective.

First, if you add only brown things (dried leaves and cornstalks, for example), it will take a long time to disintegrate. Adding greens (kitchen wastes, grass clippings, etc.) and mixing them with the browns will heat the pile to steaming in very short order. Also stirring the pile allows air to reach the center, which speeds the chemical reaction that breaks it down. You can also add a little soil to it occasionally, which provides millions of microorganisms - the key to the process.

While we once had three piles of compost working, now we have only one or two in progress. One pile is getting the greens and browns added often. The second pile, the working pile, gets stirred often. The third one becomes compost as it rests and gets used often. We stir it into new planting beds, or use as mulch, or put a little in houseplant pots, use it as winter covering for delicate plants, etc. It constantly improves the soil on our property.

A tip for gathering kitchen waste. We have a plastic compost bucket under the sink for kitchen wastes (greens). It has a lid with a latch that keeps the lid tight. We buy compostable bags that fit the bucket so that when it's full, you just pull out the bag and all and put in the pile. Add a clean bag and repeat. What can you include in the bucket? Orange peels, celery, tea bags, rotten apples, corn cobs, dead flowers, peels, egg shells (for calcium), old houseplants, etc.

Nowadays lots of things are compostable that weren't years before. Keep your eyes open. Imagine how much smaller your weekly trash will be. Combined with recycling, we now have one trash container, and put it out every other week, sometimes every third. Makes us feel good to know how much we have reduced our waste in the landfill.

When the compost is finished, it is brown and sweet-smelling. It's a beautiful, soft, crumbly brown texture, much lighter than the soil we have, and the plants love it.

One other thing - and this is for the ladies. Your husband will probably like working the compost. Let him have a go at it. My husband is the compost guru. I should buy him a T-shirt!

INDEX

CPSIA information can be obtained
at www.ICGtesting.com
Printed in the USA
BVHW081942170322
631641BV00001B/173

9 781663 221032